After Christendom?

How the Church Is to Behave If
Freedom, Justice, and a Christian
Nation Are Bad Ideas

Stanley Hauerwas

Abingdon Press
NASHVILLE

AFTER CHRISTENDOM?

Library of Congress Cataloging-in-Publication Data

HAUERWAS, STANLEY, 1940–
    After Christendom? / Stanley Hauerwas.
        p.   cm.
    ISBN 0-687-00929-4
    1. Church and the world. 2. Christianity and culture. 3. Christian
    ethics—Methodist authors. 4. Secularism. 5. Christianity—20th
    century. I. Title.
BR115.W6H38   1991
261—dc20
                                                                                91-24089
                                                                                CIP

To Stuart C. Henry
A friend who never gives advice
but in the refraining teaches me how to live.

The author gratefully acknowledges permission to reprint excerpts from:

The New Revised Standard Version of the Bible, © 1989 by the Division of Christian Education of the National Council of Churches of Christ in the USA. *A Theology of Liberation,* by Gustavo Gutiérrez, 15th Anniversary Edition © 1988, used by permission of Orbis Books and SCM Press (the footnotes refer to the original edition © 1972). *Three Rival Versions of Moral Enquiry: Encyclopedia, Genealogy, and Tradition* by Alasdair MacIntyre © 1990 by the University of Notre Dame Press. *Whose Justice? Which Rationality?* by Alasdair MacIntyre © 1988 by the University of Notre Dame Press. *The Politics of Representation* by Michael J. Shapiro © by the Board of Regents of the University of Wisconsin system. *Christian Spirituality,* by Wolfhart Pannenburg © 1983 by Wolfhart Pannenburg. Used by permission of Westminster/John Knox Press. "Scalia Missed Point but Made Right Argument on Separation of Religion" © 1990, Washington Post Writers Group. "Columbus Day," originally published in *Columbus Day* by West End Press, © 1983 by Jimmy Durham. "Religious Belief and the Constitutional Order" by William Bennett. In *Religious Beliefs, Human Rights and the Moral Foundation of Western Democracy,* ed. Carl H. Esbeck, © 1986 by the Curators of the University of Missouri. "The Priority of Democracy to Philosophy" by Richard Rorty in *The Virginia Statute for Religious Freedom,* ed. Merrill Petersen and Robert C. Vaughan, © 1988 by Cambridge University Press. Chapter 3, "The Politics of Freedom: Why Freedom of Religion Is a Subtle Temptation," is a revision of "Freedom of Religion: A Subtle Temptation" by Stanley Hauerwas, originally published in *Soundings,* an interdisciplinary journal.

99 00 01 02 03 04 05 06 07 08 — 13 12 11 10 9 8 7 6 5 4

MANUFACTURED IN THE UNITED STATES OF AMERICA

Contents

Preface

After Christendom? did not exactly "fall stillborn" from the press, but I have nonetheless regarded it as a failed book or, at least, a deeply misunderstood book. Perhaps a better way to put the matter is that *After Christendom?* got lost amid the other things I have written. I am, therefore, extremely grateful to Abingdon Press for making the book available with this new Preface. Of course, to allow an author to write a new Preface explaining why his book was misunderstood is usually a mistake. It is like a poet trying to explain a poem in prose. Such explanations are surely a sign that something is wrong with the poem.

I do not think *After Christendom?* is a "perfect" book, but I do think it is a good book that I hope will continue to be read. That *After Christendom?* was misunderstood is due in part to its publishing history. *After Christendom?* was published two years after *Resident Aliens*. Many who read *After Christendom?* as a sequel to *Resident Aliens* were disappointed by the complexity of the argument in the new book. It was not clear for some how *After Christendom?* extended the analysis offered in *Resident Aliens. After Christendom?* was not meant to be, however, a sequel to *Resident Aliens.* Rather, it was (to borrow a Hollywood term) the "prequel." *After Christendom?* was my attempt to develop the theological politics (a characterization of my position I learned from Arne Rasmusson in his *Church as Polis,* University of Notre Dame Press, 1995) necessary to sustain the call Will Willimon and I had made in *Resident Aliens* for the church to be the church.

Yet the publishing history of *After Christendom?* is not sufficient to explain the misunderstandings surrounding the book. As I note in the Introduction, *After Christendom?* is a strange mixture of theology, social and political theory, and what I call high culture journalism. Accordingly it is not clear what genre this book belongs to—which, of course, is part of the problem, but a problem I think unavoidable. *After Christendom?* represents my attempt to find a way to do theology that breaks out of the religious ghetto. Unfortunately the disciplinary character of theology shaped by seminary cultures has meant that theology is written primarily for other theologians. In short, theology has become another professionalized discipline. When theology is thus disciplined it easily loses its intelligibility as a practice within and for the church.

After Christendom? was my attempt to defy the disciplinary character of academic theology. Of course, this is not a new project for me, but in this book I tried not just to talk about how we might do theology as a politics but to do it. Accordingly I tried and continue to try to force myself as well as my readers to rethink what they normally mean by "politics" as well as what we mean by "theology." The book requires the reader to submit to a discipline, the kind I try to exemplify in chapter 4, not unlike the discipline required to learn to lay bricks or to worship God. Just as learning to speak a new language is necessary to learn to lay brick so we must learn again how to speak as Christians. One of the great problems, of course, is that many of the words used in Christian speech have become common. As a result, too often we have lost the oddness of Christian speech because we assume we are adequate speakers because such language is so familiar. The challenge is to rediscover how what we say as Christians forces a reconfiguration of our lives in order that we might see the world as God's good creation.

Take, for example, the word *church*. We usually think we know what we are talking about when we say "church." In the first chapter I try to unsettle that assumption by making us reconsider the claim that outside the church there is no salvation. That claim could be put less offensively; that is, *without* the church there is no salvation. Yet offense is often a useful way to help ourselves recover the unavoidability that Christianity names an account of the world that depends on witnesses. Accordingly the church is not simply a "voluntary association" that may be of some use to the wider polity, but rather is that community constituted by practices by which all other politics are to be judged.

Of course such a strategy is also designed to make us reconsider what we mean by politics. Politics in our society is often associated with bargaining between interest groups necessary to secure a relatively fair distribution of resources. Such an understanding of politics is what we should expect in a society shaped by liberal theory and practice. In contrast I try to help us see that politics is about the way we learn to speak about ourselves and the world. Accordingly the church must be understood as an alternative politics to the politics that so dominate our lives.

Which explains why those who describe my position as "sectarian" are at once partly right and partly wrong. They are wrong just to the extent they accept the politics that produces the description "sectarian." I certainly am not suggesting that Christians must "withdraw" from the world. Yet those who describe me as "sectarian" are right to sense that I am trying to find ways for Christians to recover the church as the locus of habits of speech to sustain our lives in service to the world. For that to happen the church must be reclaimed from the politics of liberalism that would make the church part of the "private" realm. In short the challenge before us as Christians is to be a politics that is an alternative to the politics of exchange that otherwise dominates our lives.

Rather than recommending a withdrawal strategy, the position I develop in *After Christendom?* is closer to those that would have Christians "take over" the world. Gerald W. Schlabach, a Mennonite theologian and ethicist who teaches at Bluffton College, recently sent me the criticisms that another Mennonite had posted about me on an e-mail forum. The critic had argued that my work was far too Catholic and, thus, incompatible with an Anabaptist perspective: "Hauerwas has a Constantinian fear of Christian liberty. He wants the clergy to tell us the story and the church to have the sanctions to enforce it." In his commentary, Schlabach agreed that this is an accurate (though insufficiently nuanced) summary of my views, but defended my position nonetheless. As Schlabach put it,

> Hauerwas has discovered a dirty little secret—Anabaptists who reject historic Christendom may not actually be rejecting the vision of Christendom as a society in which all of life is integrated under the Lordship of Christ. On this reading, Christendom may in fact be a vision of shalom, and our argument with Constantinians is not over the vision so much as the sinful effort to grasp at its fullness through violence, before its eschatological time. Hauerwas is quite consistent once you see that he does want to create a Christian society (polis, societas)—a community and way of life shaped fully by Christian convictions. He rejects Constantinianism because "the world" cannot be this society and we only distract ourselves from building a truly Christian society by trying to make our

nation into that society, rather than be content with living
as a community-in-exile. So Hauerwas wants Catholics to
be more Anabaptist, and Anabaptists to be more Catholic,
and Protestants to be both, and the only way he can put
this together in terms of his own ecclesial location is to be
a "Catholic" Methodist in roughly the way that some
Episcopalians are Anglo-Catholic.

That is exactly the ecclesial position that I hope *After
Christendom?* exemplifies. Of course I think this is a position that any Methodist should hold because Methodism
only makes sense as an evangelical movement in the
church Catholic. Therefore even Augustine, as I try to
show in chapter 1, can become a resource this side of
Christendom to help us discover the shape the Christian
community must take if we are to confidently live as God's
people. For the crucial divide in our time is not—as is
often claimed—between modernity and postmodernity,
but rather when the church is no longer able to shape the
desires and habits of those who claim to be Christian. In
other words modernity as well as postmodernity but names
the development of social orders that presume that God
does not exist or even if God exists we must live as if God
does not matter.

The challenge, quite simply, is how we as Christians can
narrate such a world on our terms rather than the world's
terms. That is why the last chapter of *After Christendom?* is
crucial for understanding the book. Christian educational
practices in modernity have not been able to produce
knowledges that are "ours." So we tell the story of "the West"
the way that story has been constructed by those whose purpose is to make the church and the God the church wor-
ships a minor or even negative character in the larger story
of "freedom." Does this mean that I think the way Christians
do "history" might differ from the way those who are not
Christians do "history"? The answer is an emphatic "yes."

The problem is not in the answer but that we have so few exemplifications of what such a history might look like.

That comment, however, provides an occasion for me to correct an impression my criticism of Gustavo Gutiérrez in chapter 2 might have made. I suggest that Gutiérrez, at least in *A Theology of Liberation,* might have accepted a view of liberation far too determined by Enlightenment presuppositions rather than by the gospel. I have not changed my mind about that. But I should have been clearer that in his subsequent work, particularly in his magnificent book *Las Casas: In Search of the Poor of Jesus Christ* (Maryknoll, N.Y.: Orbis Books, 1992), Gutiérrez has developed a quite different story. For as my late colleague Fred Herzog observed, the center of *Las Casas* is not Las Casas but the people Las Casas served. Gutiérrez's great achievement in *Las Casas* is to have written a biography about the triumph of the poor in Christ in a nonheroic form.

Gutiérrez's *Las Casas* is the kind of history Christians must produce if we are to tell truthfully the stories of God's work among us. Gutiérrez observes in *Las Casas* that

> a power held in the present tends to make provision for the future as well, by dominating the past of the vanquished. A people afflicted with amnesia are an unstable people, subservient to the idols of the status quo, vulnerable to the self-serving, mendacious word. Conquerors always try to erase or block the memory of those whose necks they have bent. (p. 413)

In short, "history" often becomes an exercise in amnesia just to the extent that the wrongs of the past are forgotten or made part of a plot that suggests "everything has worked out for the best." What else can you do when what has been done is so wrong there is nothing that can be done to make it right. For Christians, Gutiérrez rightly maintains, the ability to write truthfully of the suffering of the poor comes from our being made part of a history of penance and forgiveness that frees us from the need to provide self-righteous justifications for wrongs done. As Gutiérrez puts it,

> The Christian manner of assuming this responsibility is to beg humble forgiveness from God and the victims of history for our complicity, explicit or tacit, past and present, as individuals and as a church. To ask to be forgiven expresses a will to change in our behavior and reasserts the obligation of being an efficacious sign in the history of the Reign of love and justice. (p. 457)

My only reservation about Gutiérrez's claim is I think the church seldom has "a will to change," but rather righteousness is forced on us by a gracious God. "Will," at best, names our willingness to accept what is given. That is what I think is happening to the church in America. We are dying from our accommodationist strategies to be a successful church in America. But in that dying we are rediscovering possibilities of faithfulness we otherwise could not have imagined—possibilities as simple as realizing that as Christians, Las Casas and the people Las Casas served are part of our story. They are such not because we must masochistically find our identity through victimization. In the long run such a strategy only invites deeper resentment and, even worse, denigrates the assumed "victims." Rather, Las Casas narrates us because our story is God's story of God's church in the world.

I believe God is about forcing the church in America to rediscover we are God's church. *After Christendom?* is an attempt to assemble some reminders of what it would mean for the church to be free in America. Accordingly I attack notions of justice and freedom in chapters 2 and 3 that I believe are not appropriate to the kind of Christian practice I develop in chapter 4. Of course that does not mean that Christians do not care about justice and freedom, but we must be vigilant that the justice for which we call and hopefully practice is not that derived from practices that deny God's justice.

The chapter on sex and marriage may appear as something of an anomaly for a book about "politics." Why sex as a topic in a book that deals with issues like justice and freedom? Yet I hope the chapter makes clear that few issues are more political than sex and marriage. Indeed I think no aspect of our lives is more politically significant than our being a people who live lives capable of having and raising children as gifts. I hope, moreover, that this chapter can forestall an understandable but I think mistaken reaction to my position. That is, some may think that even if I am right in principle, they cannot imagine what it would mean to live the radical lives I suggest we must live as Christians. By calling attention to our commitment as Christians to live faithful in our marriages as well as be capable of welcoming children, I hope to show how Christians are already living extraordinary lives.

Grady Scott Davis has understood me better than most when he observes in his *Warcraft and the Fragility of Virtue: An Essay in Aristotelian Ethics* (Moscow, Idaho: University of Idaho Press, 1992) that

> it is in coming to grips with the constitutive institutions of the community—marriage, family, religion, political participation, and health care, for example—that the limits of the contractarian tradition become clearest and Hauerwas's writings on these topics more telling in their critical implications than even the best of Rawls' more "philosophical" critics. (p. 25)

I have no interest in being better than even the best of Rawls' philosophical critics, but I do want to help Christians discover why our commitment to being faithful to one another for a lifetime is a politics inseparable from our being a people capable of speaking truthfully to one another and to the world.

One of the reasons that *After Christendom?* may not have had the effect I should have liked is because I failed to spell

out in the book why the title ends with a question mark.
The question mark is to indicate that in *After Christendom?* I
am raising problems for which I have no solution. That I
must do so cannot help frustrating my reader, just as it frustrates me. For example, the quotation from Oliver
O'Donovan in the first chapter suggests that the justification of the nation-state in liberal political theory has been
unable to account for the natural determinants that right-
fully constitute a governable society. Accordingly the
nation-state in liberal practice has by necessity been imperialistic exactly because it denies place in the name of rep-
resenting universal ideals. I think O'Donovan's analysis of
this aspect of the modern nation-state is right, but I have no
alternative theory of society or state to propose. For me the
problem is not the absence of an alternative, but rather to
discern how Christians must learn to negotiate the false
universalism the modern state represents. Such universalism is particularly tempting for Christians because it is easily confused with Christian "homelessness."

Or to argue, as I do, that questions surrounding the relation between church and state in America are constitutionally and politically irresolvable will not sound like good
news to many. How then do we go on in a "multicultural
society?" My answer is very simple—we go on by going on.
That, moreover, is not a bad way for Christians to have to
learn to survive in a world they once thought was "theirs."
Indeed it is my hope that the Christian recognition that the
world is not ours, that the world cannot be made safe, that
there are no solutions, may make us the imaginative people
God has called us to be. Learning to live without answers,
learning to live after Christendom, Christians will hopefully discover ways to survive that may be not only surprising
for our own lives but also of service to our non-Christian sis-
ter and brother. Given the God we worship we have no reason to expect less.

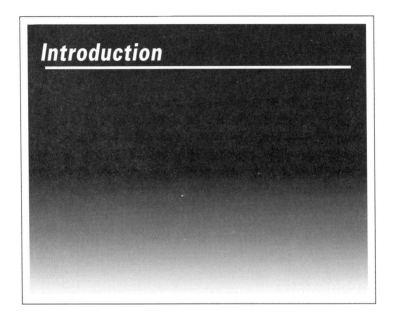

Introduction

It is not clear that given the content of this book that I should be able to write it. I am in a situation not unlike that which MacIntyre describes in his Gifford Lectures, *Three Rival Versions of Moral Inquiry: Encyclopedia, Genealogy, and Tradition.* He notes the very attempt to develop arguments against Enlightenment presuppositions by the use of the lecture as a genre is to mismatch "form and content, to deliver what one has to say over to a form well designed to prevent one saying it or to prevent one being heard saying it."[1] For the lecture makes it appear that what you have to say can be laid out in the rational style characteristic of the rational presuppositions of the Enlightenment that MacIntyre is trying to defeat.

I not only have the same problem with this book that MacIntyre had; my situation may even be worse. For I must write as a theologian who argues that Christian discourse must first be written by Christians for Christians. Yet this book originates by my being invited to deliver the New College Lectures at the University of New South Wales in Australia. New College is an Anglican institution, but the lectures are designed to address the whole university, which is not in any manner identified with Christian presuppositions and/or practices. So I must, as a Christian, try to at once speak from within the practice of the church to a wider audience, Christian and non-Christian, and yet speak intelligibly to both. Moreover, I must do that in Australia, a society that I do not know well.

The lectures I delivered in Australia as well as the fact of this book being published both in Australia and America seems therefore to put me in a peculiarly awkward position given the stance I develop in this book. For if the lectures and/or the book are successful, that seems to confirm an account of rationality and cosmopolitan presuppositions that the book is meant to challenge. In other words, the very conditions of success in the communication of the substance of what I have to say seem to contradict the content of what I am saying.

I simply have to acknowledge that in fact there is no way of avoiding this awkward position; I do not want to avoid it. The call to acknowledge the significance of the church that is the hallmark of this book does not require an intellectual or social retreat. Rather the awkward position in which I believe the church and, thus, I am in requires that we serve liberal societies by challenging their alleged universalism and cosmopolitanism.

In that respect I do not want to make too much of the difference between Australia and the United States. They are obviously in many ways quite different and in many ways similar. It would be presumptuous of me to try to characterize for Australians how they feel different from those of us who call ourselves Americans.[2]

However, both societies are fundamentally formed by Enlightenment presuppositions though in quite different ways. If Locke is the philosopher of America, Bentham and the utilitarians seem to have determined political discourse in Australia.

I must admit in many ways I prefer Australian secularism to that of America. For one of the things that is so refreshing about Australian social and political life is the absence of any abiding civil religion. No one in Australia talks about being the kind of society that will be a "beacon of hope" for the whole world. Yet Australia, like the United States, is a society that is formed fundamentally by presuppositions that can only be called liberal. As a result, I think the issues raised in this book are equally relevant to both contexts. For even though Australia is a "younger" society than America, in many ways it is a far more mature version of the project of modernity than the United States has yet to become. America continues to rely on religious presuppositions for its public ethos that cannot be acknowledged. Australian Christians are, thus, in a less awkward position than those in the United States, since Christianity never had the status in Australia as it did in America.

Our Purpose

This book challenges liberal intellectual and political presuppositions by providing an account of the power and truthfulness of Christian convictions. In brief, I argue that Christian adherence to foundationalist epistemologies—that is, the kind of position we find exemplified in thinkers such as Kant—was commensurate with social strategies of Christendom. Such social strategies were the attempt by Christians to create societies in which it would be possible to think that

Christians believed what anyone would believe upon
reflection. Ironically, this strategy turned Christianity
into a set of beliefs to legitimate the false universalism of
liberalism. In this book I challenge that strategy by
reasserting the significance of the church as the
embodiment of the necessary practices to sustain
Christian affirmation of God as Trinity.

On the surface one might well wonder what could be so
radical about such a claim. After all, it is usually
acknowledged that there must be some connection
between knowledge of God and the church. Yet I argue
that this is not simply an accidental relation but a necessary
one—outside the church there is no saving knowledge of
God. This is not a claim that most Christians wish to
acknowledge, sensing that such a claim may well put
Christians in tension with their surrounding society. If this
book serves no other purpose, it will make clear that
questions of the truth or falsity of Christian convictions
cannot be separated from how the church understands its
social and political stance.

I have learned that there is simply nothing I can do to
prevent my position from being characterized as fideistic
and/or sectarian. That these characterizations presuppose the epistemological and social positions I am
challenging does little to quiet the criticism.[3] However, I
try another tact that must also help clarify what I am
attempting in this book.

Michel de Certeau, in his *The Practice of Everyday Life*,
makes an interesting distinction between strategies and
tactics. By strategy he means any

> calculation (or manipulation) of power relationships that
> becomes possible as soon as a subject that will empower (a
> business, an army, a city, a scientific institution) can be
> isolated. It postulates a *place* that can be delimited as its

own and serve as the base from which relations with an *exteriority* composed of targets or threats (customers or competitors, enemies, the country surrounding the city, objectives and objects of research, etc.) can be managed. As in management, every "strategic" rationalization seeks first of all to distinguish its "own place," that is, the place of its own power and will, from an "environment." A Cartesian attitude, if you wish: it is an effort to delimit one's own place in a world bewitched by the invisible powers of the Other. It is also the typical attitude of modern science, politics, and military strategy.[4]

The establishment of a strategy, de Certeau notes, is accompanied by certain effects. For example, strategy provides for a triumph of place over time insofar as it allows one to acquire advantages, to prepare for future expansions, and in general to create an independence against contingency. Second, it provides for a mastery of places by making possible a panoptic practice so that foreign objects can be observed and measured and thus "included" within the scope of the vision.[5] Third, strategy is legitimated by a certain power of knowledge so that certain uncertainties of history are transformed into what de Certeau calls "readable" spaces. "Thus military or scientific strategies have always been inaugurated through constitution of their 'own' areas (autonomous cities, 'neutral' or 'independent' institutions, laboratories pursuing 'disinterested' research, etc.). In other words, *a certain power is the precondition of this knowledge* and not merely its effect or its attribute. It makes this knowledge possible and at the same time determinative characteristics. It produces itself in and through this knowledge."[6]

In sharp contrast to a strategy, a tactic, according to de Certeau, is a "calculated action determined by the absence of a proper locus. No delineation of exteriority, then, provides it with the conditions necessary for autonomy. The space of a tactic is the space of the other, thus it must play on and with the terrain imposed on it and organized by the law of a foreign power."[7] Tactic does not have power to plan a general strategy or to view the adversary as a whole. It must operate in isolated actions taking advantage of opportunities without a base where it can build up stockpiles for the next battle. It has mobility, but it gains mobility only by being willing to take advantage of the possibilities that offer themselves at given moments. As de Certeau notes, the tactic is the art of the weak.

By employing de Certeau's distinction I think of the church as tactic, not strategy. I take it that the failure to understand this is why so many react so negatively to the general position. For example, the claim that "outside the church there is no salvation" is often taken to be exclusionary. But to hear it in that fashion is to assume that the church is a strategy. To hear it in that fashion continues to presuppose a Constantinian set of presumptions that the church should determine a world in which it is safe. But I do not accept those presuppositions, because I think that the church always exists, if it is faithful, on foreign or alien grounds.

That is why I find it so odd to be accused of justifying a "withdrawal" of the church from social engagement. How can the church possibly withdraw when it, by necessity, must always find itself surrounded? There is no place to which it can withdraw. I am not asking the church to withdraw, but rather to give up the presumptions of Constantinian power, particularly when those take the form of liberal universalism.

Constantinianism is a hard habit to break. It is particularly hard when it seems that we can do so much good by remaining "in power." It is hard to break because all our categories have been set by the church's establishment as a necessary part of Western civilization.[8] Note how often both the left and the right in contemporary Christian theology continue to assume that set of presumptions. And, of course, it is exactly those presumptions that I am attempting here to call into question.

I write this book with hope that it will help us better understand our situation as Christians today and to lead that situation in a positive and constructive manner. As with so much of my past work, the book is a strange mixture of theology, social and political theory, and what might be called high-culture journalism. I am aware that this makes reading my books difficult for many, but I simply do not believe that theology can be done as if our social and political considerations are an afterthought. The very idea of systematic theology was a result of a church with hegemonic power that belied the very substance that made it church to begin with.

NB

The first chapter of the book is meant not only to get the reader's attention, but more importantly, to reshape the understanding of salvation that so many share. The claim that outside the church there is no salvation should make all of us think hard about what we mean by salvation. I try to show how our understanding of salvation is shaped by the social status of the church and that a decisive turn occurred in the Constantinian "settlement." I purposefully have used Augustine, who was certainly part of that "settlement," to show how Augustine's very political account of salvation provides resources to help us call into question the church's accommodation to our world.

The next two essays are what my students like to describe as "clearing the swamp" arguments. They are not meant to be constructive, but rather to challenge presuppositions which are so deeply held that we seldom notice their power over our lives. By challenging presumptions about the nature of justice, and indeed even whether justice ought to have the kind of priority it does in our reflection, I hope to free our imaginations to recover the significance of the gospel as the social alternative. The essay on freedom of religion is the only essay that was not part of the original design of the book. It did not seem appropriate for the lectures in Australia, though I hope Australians might find it still of interest. I have included it, however, for the American audience since the so-called "separation of church and state" has such a powerful hold over our lives.

Chapter 4 is really the central chapter of this book. There I try to offer a constructive account of Christian formation that will exhibit the fundamental presuppositions of the book. Often our insights lack conceptual resources to provide us with means to go on. By directing our attention to learning to lay brick, quilt, garden, and perhaps even write, I hope to give us a new way to think about what it means to be Christian. There my debt to Alasdair MacIntyre is perhaps most obvious.

The last two essays of the book are meant to provide concrete specifications of the kind of suggestions I have made in chapter 4. No issue more dominates the contemporary church than questions of sex. I have tried to reconceptualize those issues in a way that hopefully will give us a way not to be trapped by the current alternatives. Oddly enough, I believe that one of the most decisive political tasks before the church is to recover the significance of singleness so that marriage might again become a free calling for Christians. To be able to do that will require great drafts of courage on the part of the church today.

The last chapter on education deals with some of the most controversial issues before the church. Knowledge is not only power, but it reflects power that is often unacknowledged. I hope this essay will not only make clear how important it is for Christians to sustain their own educational enterprises, but even more, why it is important that we reconfigure what counts as knowledge. I confess that I chose the issue of "Columbus Discovering America" because I knew I would be delivering it as a lecture in Australia. I did not think it appropriate for me to try to address the issue of the Aborigines directly, but I discovered that the Australians were more than adept at renarrating my example in terms of that part of their history. The essay ends with an appendix by David Toole that challenges even further my own reading of these matters.

The fact that the book ends with a challenge should be an indication that I write without knowing the answers. I realize this frustrates many, because "good authors" are usually thought to raise problems for which they think there is a solution. It frustrates me as often as it does my readers that I have few answers. I simply cannot, by the very terms of analysis, offer an alternative to those who conceive of Christianity as a strategy. I do not apologize for that, though I do know it is frustrating.

What I do hope, however, comes through is my unrelieved excitement at what a wonderful thing it is to find one's self possessed by God and God's kingdom. In his extraordinary book *Theology and Social Theory: Beyond Secular Reason* John Milbank notes that Christianity introduced to Rome a god they could not imagine.

> Instead of Jove, the stayer of proceeding battle, Christians worship the one true God who originates all finite reality in the act of peaceful donation, willing a new fellowship with himself and amongst the beings he has created. In the "Heavenly City," beyond the possibility of

alteration, the angels and saints abide in such fellowship; their virtue is not the virtue of resistance and domination, but simply of remaining in a state of self-forgetting conviviality. Here there is nothing but "provision of peace," a condition that originally pertained also to the temporal creation, before the sinful assertion of pride and domination introduced a pervasive presence of conflict leading to death in both society and nature. But God and the heavenly Jerusalem—our "true Mother"—reached down in compassion for the salvation of the world. Salvation from sin must mean "liberation" from political, economic, and psychic *dominium,* and therefore from all structures belonging to the *saeculum,* that temporal interval between the fall and final return of Christ. This salvation takes the form of a different inauguration of a different kind of community. Whereas the *civitas terrena* inherits its power from the conqueror of a fraternal rival, the City of God on pilgrimage through this world founds itself not in succession of power, but on the memory of the murdered brother, Abel slayed by Cain. The City of God is in fact a paradox, "a nomad city" for it does not have a sight, or walls, or gates. It is not, like Rome, an *asylum* constituted by the "protection" offered by the dominating class over a dominated, in the face of an external enemy. This former refuge is, in fact, but a dim archetype of the real refuge provided by the church, which is the forgiveness of sins. Instead of a peace "achieved" through the abandonment of the losers, a subordination of potential rivals and resistance to enemies, the church provides a genuine peace by its memory of all the victims, its equal concern for all of its citizens and its self-exposed offering of reconciliation to enemies.[9]

That is the vision I hope animates this book. May we live it.

Chapter One
The Politics of Salvation

Why There Is No Salvation Outside the Church[1]

Between Establishment and Disestablishment

George Lindbeck observes that contemporary Christianity is in an "awkwardly intermediate stage of having once been culturally established but not yet clearly disestablished."[2] Awkward strikes me as exactly the right word. Most Christians, at least in the industrialized societies of the West, are unsure how we ought to think about ourselves and/or our involvement as Christians in those same societies. We are not sure whether, as Christians, we ought to or can return to times when the church at least allegedly seemed to have status if not power or whether we must seek some yet undetermined more modest stance in liberal societies.

These questions are made even more bewildering by the anomalies occasioned by sudden changes in our world. We are puzzled by the fact that in countries where we have freedom of religion it is very difficult to make serious reference to God in the public arena. Of course we are not prohibited from confessing our belief in God as long as we make the appropriate social gestures that we understand such belief has no implications for our fellow citizens who do not have such beliefs. Yet suddenly in countries that have repressed the Christian faith for most of this century, Christians, exactly because they are Christians, have become the primary political actors.[3] Indeed in those contexts it seems some even think it makes a difference, and it is a political difference, whether what Christians believe is true or false.

For many in more "democratic" countries this concern with truth almost strikes us as odd. For as Alasdair MacIntyre observed some twenty years ago, the debate between theist and atheist is increasingly culturally irrelevant and marginal. He suggested this is not due simply to the fact that secular disciplines are advancing in areas in which no direct confrontation with theism occurs. The problem is not the direction in which secular knowledge is advancing, but "the directions in which theism is retreating. Theists are offering atheists less and less in which to disbelieve. Theism thereby deprives active atheism of much of its significance and power and encourages the more passive theism of the indifferent." [4]

The "retreat" of which MacIntyre speaks is aptly indicated by the very use of *belief* to characterize what makes Christians Christians. That the question of the truth or falsity of Christian convictions is occurring in societies in which Christianity was socially and politically condemned is surely not accidental. For in such societies the continued existence of Christianity became a political challenge reminding us that all questions of truth and falsity are political.[5] In contrast, the cultural establishment of Christianity in liberal societies necessarily forced Christians to divorce their convictions from their practices so that we lost our intelligibility as Christians.

By being established, at least culturally established in liberal societies, it became more important that people *believe* rather than be incorporated into the church.

Of course the very description *established* is fraught with ambiguity, particularly in liberal social orders. Where one has separation of church and state it is often assumed that Christianity has been disestablished. The irony is, however, that Christian self-understanding of legal disestablishment presumed the continued social and cultural hegemony of generalized Christian presuppositions. You do not need an established church when you think everyone more or less believes what you believe. Particularly "awkward" in our situation is the very characterization of Christianity as a system of beliefs that was a correlative of our cultural establishment in liberal societies. This characterization robs Christians of the resources necessary to reclaim for ourselves why we believe being Christian has to do with the power that moves the sun and the stars.

In his magisterial book *Sources of the Self: The Making of the Modern Identity*, Charles Taylor notes that the crucial change in modernity is that "even in societies where a majority of people profess some belief in God or a divine principle, no one sees it as *obvious* that there is a God."[6] This loss of "obviousness" does not arise, as is often alleged, from science and education. Rather "our sense of the certainty or problematicity of God is relative to our sense of moral sources. Our forebearers were generally unruffled in their belief, because the sources they could envisage made unbelief incredible. The big thing that has happened since is the opening of other possible sources. Secularization doesn't just arise because people get a lot more educated and science progresses. This has some effect, but it isn't decisive. What matters is that masses of people can sense moral sources of a quite different kind, ones that don't necessarily suppose a God."[7]

It is my thesis that questions of the truth or falsity of Christian convictions cannot even be addressed until Christians recover the church as a political community necessary for our salvation. What Christians *believe* about the universe, the nature of human existence, or even God does not, cannot, and should not save. Our beliefs, or better our convictions, only make sense as they are embodied in a political community we call church. Taylor is quite correct that our sense of God, our very understanding of God, is correlative to moral sources, or as I would prefer, practices. For Christians, without the church there is no possibility of salvation and even less of morality and politics.

For example, I will argue in a later chapter that Christian reflection about "sexual ethics" is a hopeless mess because we have allowed the terms of the discussion to be set by presuppositions antithetical to Christian practices. To ask "Is premarital or extramarital sex legitimate?" is to have lost the day. The very notion of pre-marital sex is not a description Christians should endorse since Christians believe all sex is marital. Christian concern for sexual behavior outside the publicly acknowledged marriage has been a fear that the resulting privatization of sex would have insufficient resources to resist forms of domination that sex invites. I hope to show the significance of such moral issues are at the heart of what it means to confess that God is worthy of worship. For Christians do not believe certain things about God and then think such beliefs require life-long monogamous fidelity. Rather as part of our learning to be a people capable of practicing life-long monogamous fidelity we learn to worship God.

I am suggesting that as Christians we have a

responsibility to ourselves and our non-Christian neighbors to make use of this awkward time to rediscover the politics of salvation. After all, how can any politics be truthful that does not have as its *telos* the one alone who is worthy of worship? As servants of liberal regimen we resist asking such questions, suggesting as they do a return of Christian imperialism and/or theocracy.[8] Yet I am convinced if the church is necessary for salvation, such questions cannot be avoided even, or perhaps especially, in this awkward stage.

Why Ethics Is a Bad Idea

In some ways the awkward character of being Christian in our time is the result of living in an awkward time. Put simply, the very epistemological and political presuppositions that have led to the disestablishment of the church and that have turned Christianity into a set of beliefs are increasingly being questioned. We thus live in a time where Christians in the name of being socially responsible try to save appearances by supplying epistemological and moral justifications for societal arrangements that made and continue to make the church politically irrelevant.

The awkwardness of our times is perhaps nowhere better exemplified by the current enthusiasm for the development of something called ethics. As Charles Taylor observes that in the Enlightenment the belief was fostered that if we could "achieve the fullness of disengaged reason and detach ourselves from superstitions and parochial attachments, we should as a matter of course be moved to benefit mankind."[9] Thus the project of modernity is to base ethics, and correlatively our social and political institutions, on rationality qua rationality.

Of course the Enlightenment project to underwrite an independent realm called "morality" was a response to a very definite set of circumstances.

Rights, respect, and utility gained virtually exclusive priority in moral thought precisely when appeals to a wide range of assumptions and categories in the traditional ethos of our predecessor culture became more likely to generate conflict than agreement. Recoiling from Reformation polemics and the religious wars, modern ideologies and ethical theorists increasingly had good reason to favor a vocabulary whose sense did not depend on prior agreement about the nature of God and the structures of cosmos and society ordained by him. That the favored notions were abstracted from that same ethos should not surprise us. Neither should the fact that the resulting abstractions are ill-suited to interpret or explain much of the moral revulsion sustained by remnants of that ethos which still survive. Early modern ethical theorists disagreed rather little about cannibalism, bestiality, and the like. But as religious discord grew they found it necessary to devise a language in which highly contentious social and cosmological categories and assumptions would no longer be presupposed. Ethical theory, by sticking to this more austere language, drew a relatively tight circle around morality.[10]

Of course it is just this sense of ethics that Christians are called upon to embody in the interest of developing medical ethics, business ethics, professional ethics, and so on. We are asked to leave our theological convictions as much as possible behind and become casuists for liberal social orders. We become technicians for the working out of basic principles of autonomy, justice, and beneficence for the quandaries of the profession. The development of these highly formal accounts of "ethics," as Stout notes, was thought necessary to stop Christians from killing one another. Religion had to be socially and politically relegated to the newly created space called the private. Ethics now becomes an autonomous area of human behavior that can be distinguished from religion and etiquette. Just as we can only know X or Y is true insofar as we are able to divorce our knowing from any concrete tradition, so morality can now only be a correlative of an account of rationality qua rationality. It is now assumed that morality, as such, must be autonomous. The object of such morality is to create respect for autonomy of that new creature we have learned to call "the individual." "Medical ethics," "business ethics," and other "ethics" become ways to explore the quandaries such a morality necessarily creates.

There is a politics correlative to this understanding of truth and morality. Politics is no longer the ongoing conversation necessary for the discovery of goods in common. Such goods clearly do not exist. Rather, now politics is understood as the means necessary to secure cooperation between people who share nothing in common other than their desire to survive. Crucial to sustaining such politics is the distinction between the public and the private. The only area that legitimates the intervention of public authorities into our private lives is whether another's action will cause undue harm. Indeed it is unclear if we can even make sense of what it means for someone to be a public authority, or what it might mean for any of us to be a citizen.

This view of social and political order has momentous implications for those with Christian convictions. For example, George Will, one of America's most conservative political analysts, in a recent column reflected on the role of religion in the American polity. The occasion of his remarks was the decision by the U.S. Supreme Court, and in particular an opinion by Justice Scalia, a conservative justice, to uphold a law prohibiting the use of peyote by the "Native American Church." Commending Scalia for upholding the law, Will argued Scalia did not go far enough. According to Will, Scalia should have said the 1972 Old Amish decision was also mistaken. We need to return to Thomas Jefferson, the "patron saint of libertarians," who articulated the cool realism and secularism of the philosophy that informed the founders.

> A central purpose of America's political arrangements is the subordination of religion to the political order, meaning the primacy of democracy. The founders, like Locke before them, wished to tame and domesticate religious passions of the sort that convulsed Europe. They aimed to do so not by establishing religion, but by establishing a commercial republic—capitalism. They aimed to submerge people's turbulent energies in self-interested pursuit of material comforts.
>
> Hence religion is to be perfectly free as long as it is perfectly private—mere belief—but it must bend to the political will (law) as regards conduct. Thus Jefferson held that "operations of the mind" are not subject to legal coercion, but that "acts of the body" are. Mere belief, said Jefferson, in one god or 20, neither picks one's pockets nor breaks one's legs.
>
> Jefferson's distinction rests on Locke's principle (Jefferson considered Locke one of the three greatest men who ever lived) that religion can be useful or can be disruptive, but its truth cannot be established by reason. Hence Americans would not "establish" religion. Rather, by guaranteeing free exercise of religions, they would make religions private and subordinate.
>
> The founders favored religious tolerance because religious pluralism meant civil peace—order. Thus Scalia is following the founders when he finds the limits of constitutionally required tolerance of "free exercise" in the

idea that a society is "courting anarchy" when it abandons the principle stated in the 1879 ruling: "Laws are made for the government of actions." If conduct arising from belief, not just belief itself, is exempt from regulation, that would permit "every citizen to become a law unto himself."

Scalia's position is not only sound conservatism, it is constitutionally correct: It is the intent of the founders.[11]

This world, which I think we can call liberal, has become the presupposition of most Christians as well as most Christian theologians. We believed our task was to make such a world work. That Christian practice was relegated to the private realm was a small price to pay for living in societies that were peaceful. Therefore Christian theologians increasingly construed the Christian moral life in the language of love and justice, which usually meant that Christians should seek to construct societies that rightly know how to balance "freedom" and "equality."[12] In short, Christian social ethics became functionally atheistic, thus insuring, as MacIntyre indicates, the marginality of the theist-atheist debate. In the name of Christian responsibility to the "world," theologians became "ethicists" so they could be of service in liberal political regimens.

The Loss of a Liberal Justification for a Liberal Society

Yet in the most awkward manner this world—the liberal world—is beginning to come apart. For the epistemological assumptions that underwrote the liberal commitment to individual rights—the private-public distinction, the harm principles—have become problematic. Thus Richard Rorty simply declares, " 'The nature of truth' is an unprofitable topic, resembling in this respect 'the nature of man' and the 'nature of God,' and differing from 'the nature of the positron,' and 'the nature of the Oedipal fixation.' "[13] Yet Rorty does not believe that giving up attempts to ground the moral commitments of liberal society in reason qua reason means we must abandon liberal societies. For according to Rorty:

> It is central to the idea of a liberal society that, in respect to words as opposed to deeds, persuasion as opposed to force, anything goes. This openmindedness should not be fostered because, as Scripture teaches, truth is great and will prevail, nor because, as Milton suggests, truth will always win in a free and open encounter. It should be fostered for its own sake. A liberal society is one which is content to call "true" whatever that upshot of such encounters turns out to be. That is why liberal society is badly served by an attempt to supply it with philosophical foundation. For the attempt to supply such foundations presupposes a natural order of topics and arguments which is prior to, and overrides the results of, encounters between old and new vocabularies. The idea that (liberal culture) ought to have a foundation was a result of Enlightenment scientism, which was in turn a survival of the religious need to have human projects underwritten by a nonhuman authority. It was natural for liberal political thought in the eighteenth century to try to associate itself with the most promising cultural develop-ments of the time, the natural sciences. But unfortun-ately the Enlightenment wove much of its political rhetoric around a picture of the scientist as a sort of priest, someone who achieved contact with nonhuman truth by being "logical," "methodical," and "objective." This was a useful tactic in its day, but it is less useful now.[14]

Quoting Rorty, of course, is not sufficient to substan-tiate the claim that the liberal world is coming apart, but it at least indicates that the philosophical presuppositions that have underwritten liberal political practices are undergoing radical revision. In effect liberals, like Rorty and Stout, no longer believe in the justification of liberal democracies based on the philosophical strategies of the Enlightenment, but they still want liberal results. Any other alternative would entail, they fear, a return to the kind of conflicts occasioned by the assumption that religious convictions should have public and even political expression. The whole point, after all, of the philosophical and political developments since the Enlightenment is to create people incapable of killing other people in the name of God.

Ironically, since the Enlightenment's triumph, people no longer kill one another in the name of God but in the names of nation-states. Indeed I think it can be suggested that the political achievement of the Enlightenment has been to create people who believe it necessary to kill others in the interest of something called "the nation," which is allegedly protecting and ensuring their freedom as individuals. Rorty and Stout seem to suggest a more modest account of human ambitions that is extremely attractive, but one wonders if such moral modesty is capable of challenging, and in fact if it does not presuppose, our current nation-state system and the correlative assumption that war is justified in the names of such states.

Indeed one would like to know how liberals such as Stout and Rorty understand the status of nations. For as Anthony Giddens argues in *The Nation-State and Violence*, that nation-state as we know it is a remarkably different entity from the absolutist state that preceded it.[15] Whereas the absolutist state was primarily concerned with maintaining control over a territory for purposes of taxation, that nation-state, which exists in a complex of other such nation-states, is "a set of institutional forms of governance maintaining an administrative monopoly over a territory with demarcated boundaries (borders), its rule being sanctioned by law and direct control of the means of internal and external violence."[16] These modern conceptions of state power based on administrative competency fail to account for the inseparability of political experience and geographical locality.

> Western Europe's politics spring from a tradition of nation-states which have defined themselves in strictly territorial terms. But the political philosophies, which ought to offer us a conceptual structure for understanding this element of our political experience, have almost nothing to say about the territorial character of political units. On the contrary, it has been the preoccupation of European political philosophy since Hobbes, both in its liberal and collectionist traditions, to interpret society not in terms of its natural determinants, but in relation to the will, whether individual or common. This has resulted in a strange abstractness of intellectual political thought, running counter to the strongly territorial instincts of pre-reflective political activity. . . . It is hard to comprehend the point of organizing our formal political discussion in purely placeless concepts; human rights, democratic representation, ideological pluralism, etc., etc.—and treating those who want to talk about land as though they had sunk beneath the level of responsible discourse.[17]

By reasserting the significance of the church as necessary for Christian salvation I am aware that I cannot, like those who appeal to land as defining politics, appear dangerously reactionary. For example, to question the status of the liberal nation-state seems to suggest that a tribe might be as viable a political unit as the nation. Instead should we not, as Christians, be about developing the epistemological and moral resources to save the liberal project? If we did that, might we not find ourselves in a less awkward situation by showing the church still has something to offer the world? For if a nonparticularistic account of truth and morality is not forthcoming, are we not condemned to war between "local" polities?

Yet it is my contention that Christians would be ill advised to try to rescue the liberal project either in its epistemological or political form. The very terms necessary for that project cannot help rendering the church's challenge to the false universalism of the Enlightenment impotent.[18] Rather these awkward times give us the opportunity to recover the locality of Christian salvation called the church. Without the recovery of such locality, of such particularity, we will find that we lack the means as Christians to challenge those that would make war in the name of universal ideals.

The Church as God's Salvation

My suggestion that the church is God's salvation challenges many of the fundamental images that have characterized Christian accounts of salvation. For example, to call attention to the inescapability of the church is not simply another way to say that Christians believe in the inherent sociality of humankind. You do not need Jesus to discover the necessary sociality of the self and/or that we are inherently political.[19] Rather it is to say that salvation is a political alternative that the world cannot know apart from the existence of a concrete people called church. Put more dramatically, you cannot even know you need saving without the church's being a political alternative.

The political character of the salvation made possible by the church was ironically suppressed, but never lost, when the church became a political power. As Denny Weaver points out, prior to Constantine Christians saw themselves confronted by hostile powers that were personified in those who persecuted the church. Salvation, Christians assumed, was about the rescue from, as well as the defeat of, those powers. Indeed these pre-Constantinian Christians knew those powers were already defeated, which made possible their confident and joyful challenge to the pretentious power of Rome.[20]

It was the presumption of those Christians that they were participants in a grand drama of God's salvation of all creation. Salvation was cosmic, as in Christ's resurrection the very universe was storied by God's purposes. The church did not have an incidental part in God's story but was necessary for the salvation wrought in Christ. The church was not and is not a people gathered together in order to remember an impressive but dead founder. Rather the church is those gathered from the nations to testify to the resurrected Lord. Without the church the world literally has no hope of salvation since the church is necessary for the world to know it is part of a story that it cannot know without the church. With Weaver we observe that "Prior to Constantine, it was the church—the people of God—which made visible God's working in history. Since the minority church in a relatively inhospitable world could always feel itself in a precarious position and on the verge of extinction, it took faith to say God was in control of history." A careful reconstruction shows, "however, that church existed over against the world or in a state of confrontation with the world."[21]

God in Jesus has defeated the powers so that as disciples we can confidently live as a cruciform community in a world that has chosen not to be ruled by such love. Thus as John Howard Yoder suggests, "The church precedes the world epistemologically. We know more fully from Jesus Christ and in the context of the confessed faith than we know in other ways. The meaning and validity, and limits, of concepts like 'nature' or a 'science' are not best seen when looked at alone but in the light of the confession of the lordship of Christ. The church precedes the world as well axiologically, in that the Lordship of Christ is the center which must guide critical value choices, so that we may be called to subordinate or even to reject those values which contradict Jesus."[22]

If we say, outside the church there is no salvation, we make a claim about the very nature of salvation—namely that salvation is God's work to restore all creation to the Lordship of Christ.[23] Such a salvation is about the defeat of powers that presume to rule outside God's providential care. Such salvation is not meant to confirm what we already know and/or experience. It is meant to make us part of a story that could not be known apart from exemplification in the lives of people in a concrete community.

Salvation is the enacted narrative of God's ongoing care of Israel through the calling of Gentiles into the promised people. Richard Hays reminds us that the driving question for Paul is not, as we have been taught since the Reformation, " 'How can I find a gracious God?' but 'How can we trust in this allegedly gracious God if he abandons his promise to Israel? . . .' Paul's proclamation presents the righteousness of God not as some unheard of soteriological novelty, but as the manifestation of a truth attested by Scripture from the first. When he says that his message confirms the Law, he refers not to the specific commandments of the

Pentateuch, but to the witness of Scripture, read as a narrative about God's gracious election of a people.' "[24]

There is no more powerful witness to this understanding of salvation as enacted narrative than martyrdom.[25] For it was through martyrdom that the church triumphed over Rome. Rome could kill Christians but they could not victimize them. The martyrs could go to their death confident that the story to which their killers were trying to subject them—that is the story of victimization—was not the true story of their death. To Rome Christians dying for their faith, for their refusal to obey Caesar, was an irrational act. For the martyrs their dying was part of a story that Rome could not acknowledge and remain in power as Rome.

Thus the most determinative political witness the church had against Rome was martyrdom. By remembering the martyrs, the church in effect said, "You may kill us, but you cannot determine the meaning of our deaths." Rome does not get to tell the story of our lives, but rather the church claims to be the triumphant political community that knows the truth of our existence better than Rome. The church—exactly because it does not seek to rule through violence, though it necessarily manifests God's rule—triumphs by remembering the victory of the Lamb through the witness of the martyrs.

Denny Weaver recalls, however, that Rome did triumph by offering us the opportunity to rule as Rome understands rule—that is, through violence. That we took up such rule should not be surprising or even thought in itself as unfaithful. The salvation that Christians believe is ours in Christ is, after all, a narrative about the rule of God that necessarily subordinates all other narratives and their corresponding polities. Christians are always tempted toward theocracy because we believe what God has done in Israel and Jesus is the only true politics. When that witness is suppressed, salvation cannot help becoming anemic accounts of individual salvation, of "beliefs about this or that," and the church condemned to be but another community of togetherness. So by taking up Rome's project, Christians were attempting to further the kingdom through the power of this world: an understandable but disastrous strategy that confused the politics of salvation with the idea that in the name of God Christians must rule.

How to Go On: Augustine Reconsidered

What do these last claims about martyrdom have to do with the current debates about epistemological issues? Why does the "awkwardness," which might be called a loss of faith, in liberal political projects mean that as Christians we need to recover our salvation, which is found only in the church? Surely it is a mistake to try to make the church significant by depicting the problems of our social world in an overly-dramatic and negative fashion. Is it not good that Christians are not asked to sacrifice their lives in liberal societies, that martyrdom is not required? Instead all we need do is understand that our convictions are finally a matter of opinion.

There are no easy or quick answers to such questions. However, I focus the issues by calling attention to Augustine's account of the "two cities"—or rather by calling attention to how we have interpreted Augustine. By doing so I hope to show that Augustine provides some hints of how to live in our awkward times. After all, Augustine lived as we do in a time when the social and political world seemed to be coming apart. Moreover, it was Augustine who set the terms for the church to survive, if not triumph, in such a world.

That is just the problem, because Augustine has the

odd position of being claimed by some as the harbinger of the ascendancy of the church in the Middle Ages and by others as the originator of the Protestant rejection of that same church. The latter account is perhaps most determinatively stated in our day by Reinhold Niebuhr, who reads Augustine as justifying a "realist" account of church and society.[26] All is sin. The best the Christian can do is achieve the lesser evil, knowing that justice achieved will only be the basis for future injustice. The church is politically relevant only as it provides the account of our existence necessary for the creation of liberal democratic regimes that are capable of acknowledging the limits of all politics. Our awkward situation is no surprise for Niebuhr, as that is exactly the politics we should desire.

There is no doubt that Augustine's account of the worldly city invites a Niebuhr-like interpretation. Yet missing from Niebuhr's account is Augustine's equally strong insistence that the church is the only true political society, because only in the church are we directed to worship the one true God. Only through the church do we have the resources necessary for our desires to be rightly ordered, for the virtues to be rightly formed.[27]

The standard response to those who emphasize Augustine's account of the church is that such an emphasis on the church confuses the church with the city of God. The latter is not and cannot be instantiated in society or church. Yet such a reading of Augustine, a reading that is almost required by commitment to liberal social order, fails to see that Augustine does not think of the two cities as two distinct human associations. Rowan Williams has argued that Augustine is concerned about a *"redefinition* of the public itself, designed to show that it is life outside the Christian community which fails to be truly public, authentically political. The opposition is not between public and private, church and world, but between political virtue and political vice."[28]

Augustine argues in Book XIX of the *City of God* that Rome is not a commonwealth, because a commonwealth is determined by justice—that is, where each gets his or her due—and because Rome does not give God his due, Rome cannot be a society. Only the Christian community offers sacrifice to the true God, and it is a sacrifice that only Christ could make possible. "Thus if the pagan *res publica* is deficient as a commonwealth, it is not because Augustine polemically sets a standard of unattainably high righteousness of religious probity, but because a society incapable of giving God his due fails to give its citizens their due—as human beings made for the quest and enjoyment of God."[29]

For Augustine, societies devoid of the church cannot have any authentic conceptions of virtue. However, there is a virtue of sorts in such societies. The longing for public praise, for glory and a good name, gives a kind of unity and stability to existing orders. From Augustine's perspective, the success of the early Roman republics was at once cynical and theological: "the lust for glory restrains the more obvious factors making for disintegration in the state; and God elects to raise up a new empire over against the ancient tyrannies of the East, one which at least represents some kind of judgment upon the unbridled *libido denumandi* of those older systems."[30] Yet Rome remains vacuous, because such a republic—based as it is on pride—is built on disorder in which passion is restrained by passion.

It is true that Augustine thought the empirical state will be distinguished from the city of God insofar as the former will always be characterized by coercive power.[31] Though there is no compulsion in the city of God, the citizens, or pilgrims, of that city will exercise coercion, but when they do so they are not compromising with the earthly city.

> The city of God is not situated over against "the state" or a body which invariably exercises its power in a different manner from the secular arm; the difference is in the ends for which power is exercised, and the spirit in which it is exercised. In household and society, coercion is properly aimed at restoring the offender *paci unde desilverat*; and as we have been told by Augustine in XIX, 13 that "peace is indivisible," so to speak, that the *pax* of the individual soul and the *pax* of the universe are parts of a single continuum, so that attempts at peace on the lower levels without regard to the higher are doomed to disaster, it is clear enough that just rule (including, where necessary, the use of force) must aim at a peace which is not restricted only to temporary adjustments of passing convenience. [32]

Augustine seems to have thought of the *civitas*, like the household, is ideally about the education of the subjects. The family is the paradigm political community, not in the sense that the *polis* is conceived in organized and "totalizing" ways, but rather that both small and large scale communities are essentially purposive, existing to nurture a particular kind of life. Thus, in spite of Augustine's distaste for triumphalist ideologies of the Christian empire, he can still wax lyrical about the Christian emperor, "who is not afraid of sharing or delegating authority, who uses his power to point to the majesty of God, whose primary longing is to possess and rule his own soul in *ordo*, and whose motive in all he does is love and not the lust for glory."[33]

Yet the Christian ruler, even one like Theodosius I, is in an insoluble dilemma. For the city of God as such, according to Augustine, can never go to war even in self-defense. This is true even though the death of the city is of a different order than the death of an individual. The individual may find death a happy release, but the death of a state means the dissolution of those bonds of speech and meaning that make us rational and human. Yet the church cannot use war to preserve itself since she knows the true bonds of human speech are preserved in God's eternal will and the *ordo* of the universe as a whole. The church is not dependent on any human system for its survival.

> So we arrive at the paradox that the only reliable political leader, the only ruler who can be guaranteed to safeguard authentically political values is the man who is, at the end of the day, indifferent to their survival in the relative shapes of the existing order, because he knows them to be safeguarded at the level of God's eternal and immutable providence, vindicated in the eternal *civitas dei*. Politics and the art of government take on the Socratic colouring of a discipline of dying; and only so do they avoid the corruption of the *civitas terrend*.[34]

Which, of course, brings us back to martyrdom. I hope we have learned from this foray into Augustinian thought that genuine politics is about the art of dying. That places the church at cross purposes with the politics of liberalism, built as it is on the denial of death and sacrifice. As Christians we should not be surprised that polities so constructed are beginning to come apart now, having finally undermined the moral capital on which it depended but for which it equally could not account on its own terms.

As Christians we will not serve such a world well if we pretend that the church is only incidental to the world's salvation. The issue is how we can witness to God's rule through church without ruling. Augustine is surely right that the church as those who have been called out to worship God must maintain that all politics not so formed cannot be truthful—even liberal politics that claim not to be based on truth or virtue. Yet Augustine does not assume such a claim requires Christians to develop an ethic for everyone as the basis of which we might be able to determine the "best form of government."

Rather than engage in such grand projects, the church's main task is to be what we are—God's salvation. I suspect we will do that best when we are free from the presumption that the only way to survive is to try to accept the world's way of rule on its own terms. By renouncing that endeavor we may be able, as Augustine did for his time, to understand why we should not be surprised that a world and society built on the denial of God can only result in the strange combination of playfulness and violence so characteristic of our post-modern world. For I take that the ultimate pathos of our times is that we live in societies and polities formed by the assumption that there is literally nothing for which it is worth dying. The irony is that such societies cannot live without war as they seek to hide in war the essential emptiness of their commitments. If, as Christians, the church saves us from this emptiness, surely the world may see that is God's salvation indeed.

Chapter Two

The Politics of Justice

Why Justice Is a Bad Idea for Christians

Christian Enthusiasm for Justice and Its Problems

If there is anything Christians agree about today it is that our faith is one that does justice. You cannot be Christian without a concern for the poor, the oppressed, the down-trodden—generally those who suffer from gross inequities, both within and between societies. Moreover, it is not enough to try to meet the needs of the poor and oppressed. We are told that justice demands that we must reshape and restructure society so that the structural injustices are eradicated forever.

And we must do this not because we have some special compassion for the poor and oppressed but because they have claims against us—that is, rights. The appeal is to justice rather than charity, because charity presupposes that our aiding the poor might be something done from largess. Where charity might suggest that the poor should feel gratitude to those who come to their aid, justice reminds us that such aid is no more than what is required. The poor should not be made to feel they are recipients of charity, but rather they should think they are simply getting their due.

To raise any question about this general stance on the part of so many Christians is to appear to align yourself with the establishment against the disestablished and is taken by many as *prima facie* evidence of mean-spiritedness. After all, how can you be against justice without being for injustice? If there is anything we agree about today, it is that we all have rights—justice is the fulfillment of these rights. Raising questions about this enthusiasm for justice and rights among contemporary Christians is about as popular as admitting you secretly admire the Islamic revolution of Iran. Yet it is my contention that the current emphasis on justice and rights as the primary norms guiding the social witness of Christians is in fact a mistake.

At the popular level, appeals to justice have simply gotten out of hand. *Justice* has become a word people use to buttress the assertion that this or that set of circumstances is bad and needs correcting, but we seldom are given reason to know what is bad about the situation or what we ought to do about it. Of course it is terrible that people are starving in Africa, but it is not clear that we know better what is wrong about starvation or what we ought to do about it when we suggest they are suffering an injustice. They may well be suffering from an injustice, but it may be just bad luck. We need to know more about what justice means, in order to know if it makes sense to say that any victim of hunger is a victim of injustice. (Of course, if it is bad luck that does not mean, as Christians, our obligation to them is any less.[1] I must admit, however, that one of the things that bothers me about such discourse is the designation "us," meaning Christians, and "them," meaning the poor. Such language inherently presupposes that Christians have no convictions that might not make them poor. As a result we privilege our place as rich Christians who can justify our being rich because we are concerned about justice.)

General appeals to justice too often result in contradictory social strategies that offer little evidence of the integrity of Christian witness on such matters. For example, it is often claimed that the poor and women are oppressed and must be given more power in the name of justice. But such appeals involve quite different accounts of justice. Egalitarian presuppositions inform assertions of injustice to the poor in liberal societies; in contrast, more libertarian assumptions determine the kind of appeals women make against how they have been treated in this society. If you want to create a social order where everyone is provided with as much liberty as is compatible with liberty for all, it is very unlikely you will be able at the same time to sustain egalitarian social policies.[2]

For example, in *A Theory of Justice,* John Rawls develops detailed arguments for what he calls the "difference principle" as central to his account of justice. Thus he states his second principle of justice as, "Social and economic inequalities are to be arranged so that they are both (a) to the greatest benefit of the least advantaged and (b) attached to offices and positions open to all under conditions of fair equality of opportunity."[3] Such a principle obviously has the potential to require extensive institutional restructuring of any social orders.

Yet Rawls is very clear that this principle must be lexically ordered to the first principle of justice which requires "each person to have equal right to the most extensive basic liberty compatible with similar liberty for others."[4] These basic liberties, which Rawls roughly identifies with "political" liberties such as freedom of speech and assembly, freedom of thought and conscience, freedom of persons along with the right to hold (personal property), and freedom from arbitrary arrest and seizure as defined by the rule of law, cannot be qualified in the interest of institutionalizing the difference principle. As Rawls puts it, departures "from institutions of equal liberty required by the first principle cannot be justified by, or compensated for, greater social and economic advantages."[5]

That is why Rawls's in many ways quite admirable recent modifications of his theory in a pragmatic direction has been disappointing to some who were first quite taken with his position.[6] They thought Rawls was providing them with *the* theory of justice they needed to mount an effective critique of those forms of inequalities that seem so obvious. Instead it seems *A Theory of Justice,* as Rorty argues, is an apology for liberal societies that willingly create and sustain great economic inequalities in the name of protecting fundamental political liberties.[7]

Indeed it seems not to have occurred to many who have been influenced by Rawls that the very distinctions between political and economic realms intrinsic to his position is problematic. Anthony Giddens, for example, notes the very idea that there exists an economic sphere distinct from the political is the creation of modernity and derives from the same sources as the notions of sovereignty so elemental to the nature of the modern state.[8] Therefore, to argue for economic justice by balancing equality, even complex accounts of equality such as Rawls's, with liberty may only be underwriting presuppositions about social life that are incompatible with how Christians are taught to regard and care for one another. Moreover, the liberty and equality that we try to secure ironically legitimates the nation-state—which becomes, in Giddens's words, a "power-container whose administrative purview corresponds exactly to its territorial delimitation."[9]

Therefore Christian appeals to justice on behalf of the poor and needy may only reinforce those practices that are implicated in the creation of poverty in our society. This is but a reminder that the crucial question is not whether an appeal to justice is warranted, but rather, as Alasdair MacIntyre has argued, the more basic issue is "whose justice."[10] Indeed the problem is that we have taught by the Enlightenment to believe that in fact there is a concept of "justice qua justice" that corresponds to an account of "rationality qua rationality" which blinds us to the tradition-dependent character of any account of justice. Prior to any account of justice are those societal practices that make appeals to justice intelligible.

For example, MacIntyre notes that for any attempt to understand, much less criticize, Aristotle's account of justice it is necessary for us to try as much as possible to discard the standpoint of modernity. The very terms Aristotle uses to characterize justice and its corresponding vices cannot be correctly rendered into an idiom characteristic of beliefs of modernity. For example, the vices that are contrasted to justice by Aristotle are *dikaeosiene*—that is, acting to aggrandize oneself whether one deserves it or not—and *pleonexia,* which Hobbes explains as meaning "a desire of more than their share."

Yet as MacIntyre points out, Hobbes's understanding of *pleonexia* is misleading, as well as later translations into *greed* because *pleonexia* is not the name of a type of desire, but rather names a disposition to engage in a type of activity. In English we understand *greed* as the name of one motive for activities of acquisition, not as the name of the tendency to engage in such activities for their own sake. Translation of *pleonexia* as greed conceals the extent of the difference between

Aristotle's standpoint on the virtues and vices, and more especially his standpoint on justice and the dominant standpoint of peculiarly modern societies. For the adherents of that standpoint recognize that acquisitiveness is a character trait indispensable to continuous and limitless economic growth, and one of their central beliefs in that continuous and limitless economic growth is a fundamental good. That a systematically lower standard of living ought to be preferred to a systematically higher standard of living is a thought incompatible with either the economics or the politics of peculiarly modern societies. So prices and wages have come to be understood as unrelated—and indeed in a modern economy could not be related—to desert in terms of labor, and the notions of a just price or a just wage in modern terms makes no sense. But a community which was guided by Aristotelian norms would not only have to view acquisitiveness as a vice but would have to set strict limits to growth insofar as that is necessary to preserve or enhance a distribution of goods according to desert.[11]

While I do not wish to endorse uncritically Aristotle's account of justice as desert, the juxtaposition that MacIntyre affects with our modern conception is sufficient to indicate that appeals to justice as the central norm for Christian social ethics is insufficient at best. Yet if that is the case, is there any alternative?

Liberation as Justice

Liberation theology may appear to provide an alternative to these more general appeals to justice. Yet I think if we look at the classical statement of liberation theology, Gustavo Gutiérrez's *A Theology of Liberation*, many of the same problems appear.[12] By concentrating on this text I do not mean to suggest this is still the same position Gutiérrez holds, much less to suggest every form of liberation theology can be so characterized.[13] Rather I only use this text to illustrate how pervasive are the moral presumptions sponsored by the Enlightenment.

Under the heading "Christ and Complete Liberation," Gutiérrez distinguishes three different levels of liberation:

> political liberation, the liberation of man throughout history, liberation from sin and admission to communion with God. These three levels mutually effect each other, but they are not the same. One is not present without the others, but they are distinct: they are all part of a single, all-encompassing salvific process, but they are to be found at different levels. Not only is the growth of the Kingdom not reduced to temporal progress; because of the Word accepted in faith, we see that the fundamental obstacle to the Kingdom, which is sin, is also the root of all misery and injustice; we see that the very meaning of the growth of the Kingdom is also the ultimate precondition for a just society and a new man. One reaches this root and this ultimate precondition only through the acceptance of the liberating gift of Christ, which surpasses all expectations. But, inversely, all struggle against exploitation and alienation, in a history which is fundamentally one, is an attempt to vanquish selfishness, the negation of life. This is the reason why any effort to build a just society is liberating. And it has an indirect but effective impact on the fundamental alienation. It is a salvific work, although it is not all of salvation. As a human work it is not exempt from ambiguities, any more than what is considered to be strictly "religious" work. But this does not weaken its basic orientation nor its objective results.[14]

Gutiérrez seems to suggest that liberation from sin is the most fundamental form of liberation, the "total" liberation on which all other forms of liberation depend. Thus he says,

> Liberation is a precondition for the new society, but this is not all it is. While liberation is implemented in liberating historical events, it also denounces their limitations and ambiguities, proclaims their fulfillment, and impels them effectively towards total communion. This is not an identification. Without liberating historical events, there would be no growth of the Kingdom. But the process of liberation will not have conquered the very roots of oppression and the exploitation of man by man without the coming of the Kingdom, which is above all a gift. Moreover, we can say that the historical, political liberating event *is* the growth of the Kingdom and *is* a salvific event; but it is not *the* coming of the Kingdom, not *all* of salvation. It is the historical realization of the Kingdom and, therefore, it also proclaims its fullness.[15]

Gutiérrez, thus, argues that salvation cannot be protected by trying to lift it from the midst of history where people struggle to liberate themselves from slavery and oppression. Such a liberation "partakes in," is "integral to," the liberation of Christ, yet the latter is nonetheless more complete. For the salvation of Christ is a "radical liberation from all misery, all despoliation, all alienation."[16] It must, therefore, be "total."

At least one of the critical questions raised by Gutiérrez's claims about liberation is whether he has not, in the name of the salvation offered by Christ, underwritten an account of liberation that is oddly individualistic. For at times his account of liberation sounds far more like that of Kant and the Enlightenment than it does of the Kingdom established by Christ. Thus he says it is important to keep in mind that the object of the struggle against misery, injustice, and exploitation is "the creation of a new man."[17]

The liberation of the Latin American continent "means more than overcoming economic, social, and political dependence. It means, in a deeper sense, to see the becoming of mankind as a process of the emancipation of man in history. It is to see man in search of a qualitatively different society in which he will be free from all servitude, in which he will be the artisan of his own destiny. It is to seek the building up of a new man."[18]

Though perhaps not intending it, phrases such as "free from all servitude" and "artisans of our own destiny" have the ring of the Enlightenment. Thus Kant defines enlightenment as "man's release from his self-incurred tutelage. Tutelage is man's inability to make use of his understanding without direction from another. Self-incurred is this tutelage when its cause lies not in lack of reason but in lack of resolution and courage to use it without direction from another. *Sapere aude!* Have courage to use your own reason!—that is the motto of enlightenment."[19] Of course Gutiérrez can rightly object that he is not talking about liberation from "self-incurred tutelage," but liberation from unjust social, political, and economic oppression by forces and people outside the self. But yet it seems his ideal society, a society of the "new man," a society of autonomous individuals, at least draws its inspiration from this Kantian ideal insofar as we seek to be free from all servitude except, perhaps, that which we voluntarily accept.

Has Gutiérrez, perhaps unwittingly, underwritten a sense of liberation at odds with the gospel? For the salvation promised in the good news is not a life free from suffering, free from servitude, but rather a life that freely suffers, that freely serves, because such suffering and service is the hallmark of the Kingdom established by Jesus.[20] As Christians we do not seek to be free but rather to be of use, for it is only by serving that we discover the freedom offered by God. We have learned that freedom cannot be had by becoming "autonomous"—free from all claims except those we voluntarily accept—but rather freedom literally comes by having our self-absorption challenged by the needs of another. Yet the dominant account of freedom since the Enlightenment has denied such an understanding of freedom. We live in

> the age of the Kantian man, or Kantian man-God. Kant's conclusive exposure of the so-called proofs of the existence of God, his analysis of the limitations of speculative reason, together with his eloquent portrayal of the dignity of rational man, has had results which might possibly dismay him. How recognizable, how familiar to us, is the man so beautifully portrayed in the *Grundlegung,* who confronted even with Christ turns away to consider the judgment of his own conscience and to hear the voice of his own reason. Stripped of the exiguous metaphysical background which Kant was prepared to allow him, this man is with us still, free, independent, lonely, powerful, rational, responsible, brave, the hero of many novels and books of moral philosophy. The *raison d'etre* of this attractive but misleading creature is not far to seek. He is the offspring of the age of science, confidently rational and yet increasingly aware of his alienation from the material universe which his discoveries reveal; and since he is not a Hegelian his alienation is without cure. He is the ideal citizen of the liberal state, a warning held up to tyrants. He has the virtue which the age requires and admires, courage. It is not such a very long step from Kant to Nietzsche, and from Nietzsche to existentialism and the Anglo-Saxon ethical doctrines which in some ways closely resemble it. In fact Kant's man has already received a glorious incarnation nearly a century earlier in the work of Milton: his proper name is Lucifer.[21]

I am certainly not suggesting that Gutiérrez's "new man" can be identified with the Kantian man. Yet I think that Gutiérrez's rhetoric invites just that kind of interpretation. Indeed, I would suggest that to make the metaphor of liberation central or overriding as a description of the nature of Christian existence, as is done in much of liberation theology, is a mistake, given the background of much of our recent intellectual and political history. For when the metaphor of liberation determines or controls all other ways of understanding the Christian life, the distinctive witness of the church can be unwittingly lost. Why rely on the church when you can depend on the courage of Kant?

Pannenberg has argued that if the liberation theologians are to make their case, they must develop an account of justice. Thus Pannenberg argues that Gutiérrez's distinctions between the three levels of liberation assumes that

> all these conceptions of liberation complement each other, and he explicitly says they are mutually inclusive, representing only different "levels" of a single process of liberation. But what if these different phenomena have little more in common than the word "liberation." What if the conception of human history as a process of human self-liberation emerged in diametrical opposition to the Christian affirmation that human beings become free, not by themselves, but only by the spirit of Christ? How is it possible to harmonize such a conflict by speaking of "levels" in one and the same process? But Gutiérrez does not try to harmonize, he merely overlooks the problem. And he does very little to defend his assertion that there is more than merely a verbal relation between the Christian message of liberation from the power of sin by Jesus Christ and "the aspiration of social classes and oppressed nations" for their liberation. The problem is

that the aspirations of social classes and of nations who think of themselves as oppressed are not necessarily justified. Whether they are or whether their claims are excessive can be determined only by standards of justice. Only a theory of justice can establish that inequalities among individuals are inescapable and determine which of these inequalities are justified (or at least tolerable) on the basis of different individual contributions to the social system.[22]

Pannenberg notes that it is not an accident that Gutiérrez and other liberation theologians avoid any discussion of justice. For there simply is no generally accepted Christian theory of justice. It does little good, moreover, to invoke love as a substitute for justice. Love is equally vague, particularly in terms of its concrete social implications. For according to Pannenberg "it is only in connection with a concept of justice that love is concrete in a social situation. Without an idea of justice, it makes little sense to talk about 'orthopraxis' as a criterion of faith instead of doctrine. The outcry for 'orthopraxis' may primarily indicate today the easy awareness that a criterion of justice is lacking."[23] Therefore if we are to make the faithful connection between sanctification and politics, Pannenberg argues, we must in fact develop a Christian theory of social justice.

Such a theory, he suggests, is best developed in connection with a description of a particular social system and in relation to a hierarchy of that social system's values. "Such a theory would have to work out a critical description of the social system and its religious presuppositions, which, in the Christian tradition, are always rooted in history."[24] Yet Pannenberg argues that the political impact of such a Christian theory of justice will depend on the renewal of the theocratic idea only now as "the basis of a pluralistic, 'ecumenical' spirituality, leaving behind the older problem of dogmatic uniformity."[25]

What exactly is Pannenberg asking? How can you at once call for a theocratic theory of justice while seeming to underwrite the viability of secular-pluralistic societies?[26] Pannenberg observes that

> the dissolution of the traditional institutions of social life including family and marriage for the sake of promoting the emancipation of the individual leaves the individual to the fate of increasing loneliness in the midst of a noisy machinery of "communication." It is not likely that secular societies will be able in the long run to survive the consequences of the much-touted emancipation of the individual. In some parts of the world, secular culture survives because it lives off the substance of whatever in Christian tradition and morals has not yet been used up in the process of secularization. . . . Our cultural world, it seems, is in acute danger of dying because of the absence of God, if human persons continue to seek in vain for meaning in their personal lives, if increasing members fail to develop a sense of their personal identity, if the flood of neurosis continues to rise, if more and more people take refuge in suicide or violence, and if the state continues to lose its legitimacy in the consciousness of the citizens, while the cultural tradition functions according to the rules of supply at the discretion of individual demand. All these are the consequence of the absence of God. But far from indicating the death of God, they suggest, rather, that God is not neglected with impunity.[27]

Why then does Pannenberg still think it necessary to develop a theory of justice to justify Christian social ethics—particularly if in fact such an account of justice presupposes a social system that is at best atheistic? Of course, as we have seen, he is not alone in this respect.

Almost all forms of Christian social ethics assume that some account of justice is necessary if Christians are to be responsible social actors. Such accounts of justice, moreover, have the ironic effect of reinforcing state power, or more accurately, reifying a particular form of state power that Christians should rightly challenge.

Justice and the Modern State

There are no doubt many reasons why justice is so appealing to Christians; not the least of which is our increasing sense that the salvation wrought in Jesus is social and political in its very form. Jesus' salvation does not have social and political implications, but it is a politics that is meant as an alternative to all social life that does not reflect God's glory. Yet why should that politics be expressed in the language of justice? Part of the reason has to do with the church's attempt to remain a societal actor in societies that we feel are slipping away from our control. The current emphasis on justice among Christians springs not so much from an effort to locate the Christian contribution to wider society as it does from Christians' attempt to find a way to be societal actors without that action being colored by Christian presupposition. In short, the emphasis on justice functions as the contemporary equivalent of a natural law ethic. John Langan asks:

> What does Christian faith contribute to our understanding of justice? What can Jerusalem say to Athens about justice in the human city? There are two answers that are attractive in their simplicity but that are hard for a Christian working for justice in a pluralistic society to accept. The first is "everything." That is the theocratic answer. Briefly put, it comes to this. God is supremely just

and wills that all persons live together in justice and harmony. By this law and by his call to men to live in the spirit of the Gospel, by the teaching of his Church, he reveals to human societies what his justice demands of them. Christians, by understanding God's revelation, know what justice is, and by responding to this revelation in grace they realize it in the world. This answer runs into two problems. First, in a religiously fragmented world it is doubtful how acceptable such a purely theological conception of justice would be. Second, a purely theological conception of justice is confronted with the dilemma of being either so general that it requires independent principles if it is to guide social policy or so specific that it effectively canonizes for all societies and all times the norms and social structures of a primitive agricultural society or of a dissident apocalyptic minority in the Roman Empire. It seems implausible to maintain that the norms for the just operation of the Chase Manhattan Bank can be derived from consideration of the Decalogue and the Sermon on the Mount or from application of the prescriptions governing the year of jubilee. Even for those who would commit themselves to a purely theological notion of justice in society, in a spirit of confidence and trust in the Lord, the risk of being relegated to the fringes of society and losing influence on the forming of social policy remains and should remain a problem.[28]

The second answer according to Langan is "nothing." This can be based on the assumption that the human city is so corrupt it cannot be made just or that the ends of the human city are worthy but remain inferior to the end of salvation. Langan cannot accept such an answer because the Christian faith interprets the struggle for justice to be part of the history of salvation. Therefore Christians cannot help trying to find ways to express the universal desire for justice, which is the source of ideals for better political communities. Christian love motivates Christians to join with non-Christians in the search for justice in an imperfect world.

The problem with such reasoning, however, is the assumption that we share enough to even know what justice might mean. Many well-intentioned people have taken this path on the assumption that in fact we do share a general sense, if not conception, of justice in our society that allows us to work for common goals. Thus one of the primary agendas of Christian ethics has been an attempt to show how systems such as that of Rawls are an expression of or can be justified by Christian convictions.[29] Moreover, once justified we no longer need to look back to our Christian convictions but can be content with Rawls's account since we are confident that such a theory of justice provides the perspective that Christians need. But note, as Langan suggests, that if Christians are not able to share such an account of justice they may well be relegated to the fringes of society—we would not have power. We say we want justice but I suspect even more that we want power—power to do good, to be sure, but power just the same.

By introducing the importance of power, I am not trying to suggest that power is always to be avoided by Christians. Indeed, the exact opposite is the case. One of the things that bothers me about liberal conceptions of justice is the avoidance of questions of power. As R. H. Tawney noted in his book *Equality*, "Freedom is always relative to power, and the kind of freedom which at any moment it is most urgent to affirm depends on the nature of the power which is prevalent and established. Since political arrangements may be such as to check excess of power, while economic arrangements may permit or encourage them, a society, or a large part of it, may be both politically free and economically the opposite. It may be protected against arbitrary action by agents of government, and be without the security against economic oppression which corresponds to civil liberty."[30] Indeed, as we have learned since Tawney wrote, the very form of liberty itself may only hide forms of domination. The question is not whether to have or not to have power, but to what end. Liberal conceptions of justice, such as Rawls, unfortunately tend to hide from us just that kind of consideration.

This is not the place to mount a further critique of Rawls, but it should at least be pointed out that his account of justice, though surely elegant, has been subject to powerful philosophical objections. In particular, Michael Sandel argues that the moral psychology inherent in Rawls's position entails a view of the self that is essentially alienated from itself and community. "Where for Hume, we need justice because we do not *love* each other well enough, for Rawls we need justice because we cannot know each other well enough for even love to serve alone."[31] I am not suggesting that Rawls does not have some means to respond to such an objection. But even if he does, it seems odd for Christians—in their desperate search for a theory of justice—to embrace Rawls as if such issues do not matter.

No discussion of justice by Christians can ignore Michael Ignatieff's *The Needs of Strangers*. There Ignatieff argues that the problem with most contemporary political philosophies is not that they are individualistic, but that in the absence of any account of the good, individuals are led to believe that all their needs are legitimate.[32] Justice, thus construed, leads to efforts to create societies that are free of constraints upon the needs of its members. From such a perspective, liberal-capitalistic and Marxist societies are but mirror images of one another. By necessity they each have to be imperialistic. Imperialism provides the only means these societies have of satisfying the unjust expectation that they have legitimated.

From such a perspective the current debate between Rawls and Robert Nozick is basically a debate between friends. Even though Nozick—at least in *Anarchy, State and Utopia*[33]—is a libertarian and Rawls tries to justify a distributive account of justice, they share the same set of presuppositions about society—namely, society is a collection of individuals that must be convinced that it is in their interest to cooperate to some degree. Rawls tells us time and time again that the aim of a theory of justice is to make society, as much as possible, a cooperative venture for mutual advantage.

Such a view, as MacIntyre has suggested in *After Virtue,* does carry with it a certain note of realism.

> Modern society is indeed often, at least on the surface, nothing but a collection of strangers, each pursuing his or her own interests under minimal constraints. We still of course, even in modern society, find it difficult to think of families, colleges, and other genuine communities in this way; but even our thinking about those is now invaded to an increasing degree by individualist conceptions, especially in the law courts. Thus Rawls and Nozick articulate with great power a shared view which envisages entry into social life as—at least ideally—the voluntary act of at least potentially rational individuals with prior interests who have to ask the question "What kind of social contract with others is it reasonable for me to enter into?" Not surprisingly it is a consequence of this that their views exclude any account of human community in which the notion of desert in relation to contributions to the common tasks of that community in pursuing shared goods could provide the basis for judgments about virtue and injustice.[34]

So in the interest of working for justice, contemporary Christians allow their imaginations to be captured by the concepts of justice determined by the presupposition of liberal societies. For example, we simply take for granted distinctions between fact and value, public and private, that these societies privilege.

As Lesslie Newbigin has pointed out, at the core of our culture is an ideal of knowledge of what are called "the facts." These wonderful entities can become even more impressive as "data" when given particular authority through the pseudo-methodologies of the social sciences. They are allegedly quite independent of the "subjectivistic biases" of the knower. They are therefore "value-free."[35]

"Facts" create, or at least legitimate, the public world, as facts are the basis for agreement among all intelligent persons. We can enforce or require belief only about those matters that are clearly "factual." Of course, as Newbigin points out:

> The vast majority of people depend most of the time for most of their information on experts in the various fields. But this dependence implies that we trust the experts to be scrupulously honest and careful in their analysis and testing. It implies that their statements rest on evidence that we could—if we had the time and training—verify for ourselves. In contrast to this is the private world where we are free to follow our own preferences regarding personal conduct and lifestyle, provided it does not prevent others from having the same freedom. There are no "right" or "wrong" styles of life. Perhaps the only thing that is really wrong is condemning as wrong the lifestyle of another. In the field of personal values pluralism reigns.[36]

Newbigin's suggestion that, for all our belief in objective knowledge, most of us in fact now defer to experts is basically correct. But it is a mistake to think that scientific methodologies gave birth to the expert. Rather it was the necessity of liberal societies to find social mechanisms to provide for social control—bureaucracy being the seminal cause for this—that creates the necessity of facts over which experts can be authorities. For bureaucracies are built as mechanical models where a high degree of division of labor, specialization, predictability, and anonymity are meant to ensure the criterion of efficiency. As Newbigin notes, "It is the essence of bureaucracy that it sets out to achieve a kind of justice by treating each individual as an anonymous and replaceable unit. Bureaucracy applies the principles of reason as understood at the Enlightenment to human life in the public sphere: the analysis of every situation into the smallest possible components and the recombination of these elements in terms of logical relationships which, ideally, can be expressed in mathematical terms and handled by a computer. In its ultimate development, bureaucracy is the rule of nobody and is therefore experienced as tyranny."[37]

Bureaucracy is legitimated by its promise to be efficient and effective. The figure who reigns supreme in this world is, of course, the manager who is supported by social scientists. Just as theologians once were in the service of bishops, popes, and kings, now social scientists are used to legitimate our leaders who promise to be the best managers of crisis. To underwrite the authority of such experts, to ensure their predictive power, it is necessary to create the fact-value distinction. In fact we increasingly become self-interested individuals to ensure our new master's authorities for otherwise we fear anarchy. In short, it becomes a moral necessity to be greedy as otherwise we would throw people out of work, and the predictive power of economics would be even more doubtful than it already is.

Though there is no question that human behavior has regularities that make certain generalizations possible, the sources of unpredictability make the generalizations that sustain the social sciences fragile at best. Fortune simply cannot be predicted, yet it must be denied or repressed as otherwise the authority of the expert is undermined.[38] This has immense importance, of course, for the role of the social sciences in the legitimation of modern states.

> Office statistics are an invaluable source of data for social research. But they are not just "about" an independently given universe of social objects and events, they are in part constitutive of it. Other implications also derive from this. Social science, even in its earliest formulation, did not come fresh-faced and innocent to an ordered array of empirical data. The collection of official statistics is impossible without those involved having a systematic understanding of the subject matter that is the concern of those in statistics. Such an understanding is progressively monitored, in the modern state by much the same methods as "independent" social scientists use to analyze the data thus produced. From this it follows that the social sciences have themselves been persistently implicated in the phenomenon they set out to analyze. . . . Social science, in other words, has from its early origins in the modern period been a constitutive aspect of that vast expansion of the reflexive monitoring of social reproductions that is an integral feature of the state.[39]

It has become a commonplace that one of the oddities of modernity has been how societies built on claims of the freedom of the individual, with the attending distinction

between the public and private, have led to the growth of
the bureaucratic state. Of course such a state appears
noncoercive, since its task is not to compel obedience, but
rather to achieve administrative ends. The state is
putatively in existence to protect individual rights, but to
accomplish that end it is necessary to create a bureaucracy that is more intrusive than the most absolute
monarch. We are taught that each person has a right—a
claim—to life, liberty, and the pursuit of happiness, but
the question has to be asked:

> "Who is under obligation to honor the claim?" In the
> Middle Ages the answer was found within the network of
> reciprocal rights and duties. The man farming the land
> had a duty to provide troops to fight his lord's battle and a
> corresponding right to his lord's protection. Duties and
> rights were reciprocal. One could not exist without the
> other, and all were finite. But the quest for happiness is
> infinite. Who, then, has the infinite duty to honor the
> infinite claim of every person to the pursuit of happiness?
> The answer of the eighteenth century, and of those who
> have followed, is familiar: it is the nation-state. The
> nation-state replaces the holy church and the holy empire
> as the centerpiece in the post-Enlightenment ordering of
> society. Upon it devolves the duty of providing the means
> for life, liberty, and the pursuit of happiness. And since
> the pursuit of happiness is endless, the demands upon
> the state are without limit. If, for modern Western
> people, nature has taken the place of God as the ultimate
> reality with which we have to deal, the nation-state has
> taken the place of God as the source to which we look for
> happiness, health, and welfare.[40]

The same state gives us correlative notions of
citizenship and war. The mass of the population of
traditional states did not know themselves to be citizens

of those states, and it did not particularly matter to the continuity of power within them. "But the more the administrative scope of the state begins to penetrate the day-to-day activities of its subjects, the less this theorem holds. The expansion of state sovereignty means that those subject to it are in some sense—initially vague, but growing more and more definite and precise—aware of their membership in a political community and of the rights and obligations such membership confers."[41] Therefore in modern polyarchic order, citizenship rights are the "price paid" by the dominant class for the means of exercising its power. But the price for citizenship is acceptance of the obligation of military service. "Conscription was prompted by considerations of social policy as much as by military expediency. 'Military service emerged as a hallmark of citizenship and citizenship as the hallmark of a political democracy.' . . . Only with the experience of the First World War, in which conscription was not introduced until the armed forces had undergone huge losses, was universal male franchise instituted. Once more this was done in explicit recognition of the ties between citizenship rights and military obligations."[42]

It is not clear which came first—the modern state or the modern military. In the military, administrative power in its modern guise was pioneered. The military initiated those changes necessary for modern bureaucratized organization—"the formation of a body of experts holding exclusive knowledge of certain essential administrative techniques, and the simultaneous creation of a 'de-skilled' population of ordinary soldiery."[43] For example, note how our understanding of *uniform* and *discipline* are the result of this transformation. *Uniform* was originally an adjective but became a noun as standardized clothes became the norm for armies; and *discipline*, which once denoted a property of someone who followed a set of teachings came to mean the end result of such instruction. Accordingly personal displays of heroism became reduced in importance in favor the anonymity of efficient fighting forces.[44] The modern army became a microcosm of the state as a whole.[45]

In the interest of working for justice, Christians allow their imaginations to be captured by concepts of justice determined by the presuppositions of liberal societies, and as a result, contribute to the development of societies that make substantive accounts of justice less likely. Out of an understandable desire to be politically and socially relevant, we lose the critical ability to stand against the limits of our social orders. We forget that the first thing as Christians we have to hold before any society is not justice but God.

What Then Can We Do?

Does that mean we must give up working for justice in the societies of modernity—in particular if we remember that *peoples* and *society* is not synonymous with *national interests?* That is certainly not my intention. But it does mean that we must be much more chastened in our attempts to develop "a theory of justice" that will somehow give us the means to know in principle what justice qua justice entails. Generally I think modern-liberal societies lack the means to generate an intelligible account of justice. Attempts to ground justice in abstract rights and/or contractual agreements can only result in ideal theories that distort our moral capacity even further. As Christians we will speak more truthfully to our society and be of greater service by refusing to continue the illusion that the larger social order knows what it is talking about when it calls for justice.[46]

Chapter Three

The Politics of Freedom

Why Freedom of Religion Is a Subtle Temptation

Against Freedom?

It is hard to be against freedom of religion. On the face of things it seems to be such a remarkably good idea. It will be particularly hard to be against freedom of religion over the next few years as Americans celebrate the Constitution and the Bill of Rights. For all the difficulty caused by our trying to reconcile the two clauses of the First Amendment—that is, freedom of religion with the disestablishment of religion—I am sure we will be greeted with article after article reaffirming the judgment that the First Amendment is an ingenious invention for the good of state and religion alike. Religious thinkers will write learned theological treatises justifying freedom of religion as the best known means of reconciling the equally legitimate demands of church and state.

Yet I am not convinced that freedom of religion has been good for church or society in America. It has tempted Christians in America to think that democracy is fundamentally neutral and, perhaps, even friendly toward the church. American Christians, of every Protestant denomination and now also Catholics, have thought their primary religious duty to the state was and is to provide support and justification for the state that guarantees freedom of religion. Such justifications are based on the premise that America is a limited state—that is, the state is constitutionally prohibited from placing inappropriate demands on religious consciousness, so that our task as church is to support that achievement.[1] As a result, Christians in America have failed in our responsibility to this state by domesticating the gospel in the hopes of controlling, if not dominating, the ethos of this society.

A more nuanced way to put my case is not that the First Amendment in and of itself has been bad for this society and the church, but that the First Amendment, when interpreted against the backdrop of political liberalism, has had disastrous results for church and society. I do not want to take the sting out of the argument to follow, but I hope it will be clear that I am not suggesting we repeal the First Amendment. The First Amendment could be a politically significant way for a state to acknowledge those public enterprises so essential to the public weal that they should be protected from command of the government. It is the brunt of my case, however, that for a complex set of reasons the First Amendment does not serve that end in our society. Moreover, my concern is not with the failure of American society in this respect, but with the failure of the church to hold this society to be true to its own best commitments.

Because Christians have been so concerned with supporting the social and legal institutions that sustain freedom of religion, we have failed to notice that we are no longer a people who make it interesting for a society to acknowledge our freedom. Put differently, in such a context, believer and nonbeliever alike soon begin to think what matters is not whether our convictions are true but whether they are functional. We thus fail to remember that the question is not whether the church has the freedom to preach the gospel in America, but rather whether the church in America preaches the gospel as truth. The question is not whether we have freedom of religion and a corresponding limited state in America, but whether we have a church that has a people capable of saying no to the state. No state, particularly the democratic state, is kept limited by constitutions, but rather states are limited by a people with the imagination and courage to challenge the inveterate temptation of the state to ask us to compromise our loyalty to God.

Freedom of religion is a temptation, albeit a subtle one. It tempts us as Christians to believe that we have been rendered safe by legal mechanisms. It is subtle because we believe that our task as Christians is to support the ethos necessary to maintaining the mechanism. As a result, we lose the critical skills formed by the gospel to know when we have voluntarily qualified our loyalty to God in the name of the state. We confuse freedom of religion with freedom of the church, accepting the assumption that the latter is but a specification of the former. We thus become tolerant, allowing our convictions to be relegated to the realm of the private.

Though some of our founding fathers clearly desired to qualify the power of the church (and in particular the Episcopal Church) in public life, the subversion of Christianity, to use the title of Jacques Ellul's recent book, was largely unintentional.[2] The church did not experience rejection through the enactment of the First

Amendment. That would have been preferable as then at least we would have known we were in conflict. Rather, the church was subverted by being asked to support society by making the gospel a civil religion in which the church, ironically, can only be politically irrelevant. For "insofar as individual denominations have relinquished their claims to be 'the church,' the nation itself has tended more and more to assume this function, speaking with far greater authority than purely voluntary ecclesiastical societies."[3]

That such was the case partly derives from what William Lee Miller described as the new idea that was at the heart of the American experiment—namely, "that there did not have to be any link between religion and the state, between ultimate convictions and the power of the law. The unity of the state did not require any unity of religion. A great nation-state could exist, and hold together, and walk upright upon its legs among the nations of the world, without the spinal column of an official religious institution. The variety of religious beliefs and nonbeliefs could be altogether voluntary; in the eyes of the state they could be equal and free. The mixture of beliefs in the nation could be whatever the people would decide upon."[4] Yet this formal independence of the state from religion did not entail the hostility of the state to religion. On the contrary, as Miller points out, it was thought that the very character of this new "thing" depended on the continuation of a vital religious tradition.

Justice Douglas's famous quotation, "We are a religious people whose institutions presuppose a Supreme Being," nicely enshrines this attitude. We may have disestablished religion legally but we by no means disestablished it culturally. Although the idea of a formal religious establishment eroded [in the nineteenth century], the assumption that there should be a religion common to the society did not fade so easily. So even though the American colonies became states which formally disestablished any particular religious tradition, they did not exclude the possibility that some more general expression of Christianity would be presumed common to the social order. Of course, in the early years of the nineteenth century it was taken for granted that Christianity meant versions of Protestant Christianity. So the denominational system that evolved in the new American nation presumed that each version was a specification of a broader dominant religion. This religion played something of the value-generating and order-ensuring role ascribed to establishments in the older territorial patterns. . . . Evidence that Protestant Christianity became the functional common religion of the society would overwhelm us if we sought it out. What is of more interest here is how observers concerned with American society simply took this phenomenon for granted.[5]

Yet, history sometimes has some sobering surprises. Now, after two centuries, the long-delayed outcome has arrived. The full complexity of "freedom of religion" is coming into view. The "long de facto Protestant establishment has clearly ended, and because no other candidate for that effectively dominant cultural-religious position can successfully take its place—not any other religious persuasion, not any combination of religious groups, but also not, despite the noisily articulated fears of segments of the conservative religious community, 'secular humanism' either. Establishment by law ended in the nineteenth century. Establishment by cultural domination ended in the twentieth."[6]

The end of a religious establishment reminds us that

the larger issue behind granting freedom of religion always was and is how to form a culture. If freedom of religion "solved" the problem of religious pluralism in America, it did so by leaving us the problem of forming a culture that was only intensified through the historical working out of that "solution." How are the moral underpinnings of such a culture to be formed? "Who is responsible for shaping 'Virtue' in the citizenry? How is it done? With what institutions? Supporting what ultimate convictions?"[7] That we are confronted by so large a problem is surely why Christians in such a society think they must supply a "civil or public" religion that supports the continued commitment to freedom of religion. But in the process it remains unclear how the church becomes anything more than a court religion held captive to the interests of a nation-state.

The Alternatives Before Us

In an effort to help clarify the situation I believe we confront, I am going to direct our attention to two quite different alternatives before us—one the position of philosopher Richard Rorty and the other the position of the former Secretary of Education William Bennett. By doing so I hope to uncover some of the basic philosophical and theological issues confronting the church in a society formed by the belief (and practice) that freedom of religion has basically solved questions of the relation of church and state.

I have suggested that freedom of religion has been one ingredient in our increasing tendency to be a society that is morally and spiritually empty at its core. Yet, not all think this is a negative result, but rather a profound moral achievement. For example, Richard Rorty in his paper, "The Priority of Democracy to Philosophy," begins quoting Thomas Jefferson, "It does me no injury for my neighbor to say that there are twenty Gods or no God" as the basic insight necessary to sustain American liberal politics.[8] According to Rorty, Jefferson thought that the common moral faculty shared by theist and atheist alike was sufficient to sustain civic virtue. Jefferson did not think that religious beliefs should be completely discarded, but it is enough that religion be privatized, making it irrelevant to social order but relevant and possibly even essential for individual perfection.

Rorty suggests that Jefferson's compromise concerning the relation between spiritual perfection and public policy had two sides: an absolutist side—which says that every human being has all the beliefs necessary for civic virtue based on a universal human faculty which gives every human being dignity and rights—and a pragmatic side—which says that when the individual finds in her conscience beliefs that are relevant to public policy, but incapable of defense on the basis of common beliefs, such beliefs must be sacrificed on the altar of public expedience (p. 2). It was only in the Enlightenment that the tension between these two stances was eliminated, as the Enlightenment idea of reason was based on the claim that "there is a relation between the ahistorical essence of the human soul and moral truth which insures that free and open discussion will produce 'one right answer' to moral as well as to scientific questions. Such a theory guarantees that a moral belief which cannot be justified to the mass of mankind is 'irrational,' and thus not really a product of our moral faculty at all" (pp. 2-3).

Yet Rorty notes that this rationalistic justification of the Enlightenment compromise has now been discredited by contemporary intellectual developments. Anthropologists and historians of science have blurred the distinction between innate rationality and the products of acculturation. Philosophers have increasingly argued that as humans we are "historical all the way through." As a result, some writers, such as Horkheimer and Adorno, argue that liberal cultures and institutions either should not or cannot survive the collapse of the philosophical justification that the Enlightenment provided for them. In particular it is argued that the lack of philosophical rationale for liberal societies means they cannot supply the theory or practices (habits) necessary to develop or sustain morally coherent selves.

Drawing on the later Rawls—that is the Rawls who increasingly backs away from his attempt to justify the principles of justice in a Kantian fashion—Rorty simply denies that democracy needs justification as the Enlightenment thought. Rather as heirs of the Enlightenment, for whom justice has become the first virtue, "we can be as indifferent to philosophical disagreements about the nature of the self as Jefferson was to theological differences about the nature of God" (p. 15). Quoting Rawls, Rorty argues, "What justifies a conception of justice is not its being true to an order antecedent to and given to us, but its congruence with our deeper understanding of ourselves and our aspirations, and our realization that, given our history and the traditions embedded in our public life, it is the most reasonable doctrine for us" (p. 21).[9] Therefore all Rawls meant by his earlier appeals to an Archimedean point in justification of his theory is not a point outside history, but rather "the kind of settled social habits which allow a lot of latitude for further choices" (p. 25).

According to Rorty, all this way of thinking about democracy and its guaranteed freedom requires is that figures such as Loyola and Nietzsche, who would subordinate all our ends to one dominant end, be viewed as mad. They are such because "there is no way to see them as fellow-citizens of our constitutional democracy, people whose life-plans might, given ingenuity and good will, be fitted in with those of other citizens. They are not crazy because they have mistaken the ahistorical nature of human beings. They are crazy because the limits of sanity are set by what we can take seriously. This in turn is determined by our upbringings, our historical situation" (p. 27).[10] Rorty is aware that this way of dealing with Loyola and Nietzsche may seem shockingly ethnocentric to those accustomed to the idea that anyone willing to listen to reason can be brought around to the truth on the assumption that the human self has a center, a truth-tracking faculty called "reason." The confidence that there is such a faculty means that with time and patience argument will penetrate to such a center, assuring agreements. But Rorty argues (and in doing so claims Rawls as a fellow traveler) that such a view of the self is not needed. Rather "we are free to see the self as centerless, as an historical contingency all the way through" (p. 28).

Rorty rightly sees that the mistake of Enlightenment accounts of religious tolerance is that they have tried to provide a theory of human nature, a philosophical account, to justify such tolerance. In contrast, he sees that not every challenge must be met in the terms in which it is presented.

> Accommodation and tolerance must stop short of a willingness to work within any vocabulary which one's interlocutor wishes to use, to take seriously any topic which he puts forward for discussion. To take this view is of a piece with dropping the idea that a single moral vocabulary and a single set of moral beliefs are appropriate for every human community everywhere, and to grant that historical developments may lead us to simply *drop* questions, and the vocabulary in which those

questions are posed. Just as Jefferson refused to let the Christian Scriptures set the terms in which to discuss alternative political institutions, so we must either refuse to answer the question "What sort of human being are you hoping to produce?" or at least, must not let our answer to this question dictate our answer to the question "Is justice primary?" It is no more evident that democratic institutions are to be measured by the sort of person they create than that they are to be measured against divine commands. . . . Even if the typical character-type of liberal democracies are bland, calculating, petty and unheroic, the prevalence of such people may nevertheless be a reasonable price to pay for political freedom. (pp. 32-33)

Rorty is aware that many will find his recommendations of a "light-minded aestheticism" toward traditional philosophical questions troubling, but he claims that there is a moral purpose behind such light-mindedness. For to adopt such an attitude about philosophical topics serves the same purpose as does the same attitude toward traditional theological topics.

Like the rise of large market economies, increased literacy, the proliferation of artistic genres, and the insouciant pluralism of contemporary culture, such philosophical superficiality and light-mindedness helps along the disenchantment of the world. It helps make the world's inhabitants more pragmatic, more tolerant, more liberal, more receptive to the appeal of instrumental rationality. If one's moral identity consists in being a citizen of a liberal polity, then to encourage light-mindedness will serve one's moral purposes. Moral commitment, after all, does not require taking seriously all the matters which are, for moral reasons, taken seriously by one's fellow-citizens. It may require just the opposite. It may require trying to josh them out of the habit of taking those topics so seriously. (p. 39)

Such light-mindedness is exactly what William Bennett fears. According to Bennett, a return to the moral principles that underwrote our Constitution, and in particular religious freedom, is necessary. We must retrieve the Constitution from the lawyers so that we can reclaim the "philosophical underpinnings" that support the Constitution of the American people. Those values Bennett identifies as the Judeo-Christian ethic, the democratic ethic, and the work ethic. Bennett notes that while his upbringing has made him sympathetic to religious belief, he is not a fanatic, because he is rather average in his degree of religious observance. However, as a friend of religion he is often attacked as an "ayatollah" for suggesting that the American experience cannot be understood without reference to the Judeo-Christian tradition (pp. 1-2).[11]

Such an attack, he argues, is completely unjustified, particularly as it raises the specter of religious intolerance, thus denying the fundamental strength of the American people—namely, that we are "a people at once deeply religious and deeply tolerant" (p. 2). What must be remembered, according to Bennett, is that all our founders, divided as they were by rich diversity of religious allegiances, were "united by a common belief in the importance of religion as an aid and a friend to the constitutional order" (p. 2). Bennett cites Adams's familiar claim, "Our Constitution was made for a moral and religious people. It is wholly inadequate to the government of any other" (p. 3), in support of his contention that religion is necessary to preserve a tolerant society.

That our founders thought there was an essential connection between religion and liberty, according to Bennett, is a matter of common sense. "Our commitment to liberty of conscience—including the freedom to believe or not to believe—follows, in good part, from the respect for religion felt by the majority of Americans. It is ironic that anyone who appeals today to religious values runs the risk of being called 'divisive' or attacked as an enemy of pluralism, for the readiness of most Americans to defend tolerance and equality does not derive only from an abstract allegiance to Enlightenment ideals. It comes also from a concrete allegiance to the Judeo-Christian ethic" (p. 3).

Bennett provides two further reasons beyond this commonsense view of the founders for considering religion to be indispensable to democracy. First, religion deepens politics, as it is the wellspring of civic virtues, promoting hard work and individual responsibility, lifting each citizen outside himself by inspiring concern for community and country. Secondly, religion promotes tolerance. This seems paradoxical because religion is about absolute truth, which can lead to intolerance, but thankfully in America, this seldom happens. Indeed, in America, religion has the opposite effect. Thus, Bennett quotes President Reagan at an ecumenical prayer breakfast, saying: "Our government needs the church because those humble enough to admit they are sinners can bring to democracy the tolerance it requires in order to survive" (p. 4). (I wonder if Reinhold Niebuhr would appreciate the irony of finding his position now taken by Ronald Reagan.)

Bennett glosses former President Reagan's insight by observing that not only does religion moderate "the potentially divisive tendencies of religion. When religion is excluded from public life, it can become resentful, extremist, and sectarian. But when religion is included in public life and is subject to public scrutiny, it learns to speak in a language that all sects and all citizens can understand. As Jefferson wrote to Madison, 'by bringing the sects together . . . we shall soften their asperities, liberalize and neutralize their prejudices, and make the general religion a religion of peace, reason, and morality.' " Bennett observes, moreover, that Jefferson was right, because religious groups in a democracy—where so much depends on broad public sentiment—find that they must pursue "their ends by appealing to a consensus of shared, not particularized values. This has happened throughout American history, and it happens today" (p. 4).

Therefore, freedom of religion, which has as its primary value the support of tolerance based on absolute freedom of conscience, is the first of our freedoms. The founders saw no conflict between our individual rights and our common values. "In their minds, complete neutrality between particular religious beliefs can and should coexist with public acknowledgment of general religious values" (p. 5). Bennett argues further that this is not simply a question of constitutional principle, but social health. We are beginning to realize that many of our social problems cannot be solved without the improvement of character. "And for many of us, for most of us, religion is an important part of the development of character" (p. 5).

Thus Bennett calls for a reconstitution of the consensus of the founders who were comfortable with a public role for religion. For example, even Jefferson thought religion essential to education in order to provide moral training. Moreover, the United States Congresses saw nothing wrong with authorizing chaplaincies for the Army and Navy. Our founders knew that for the "sake of liberty, government should acknowledge the religious beliefs on which democracy depends—not one single belief but belief in general" (p. 6). In particular this means that we must tell our children the truth about our history. The story of America "is the story of the highest aspirations and proudest accomplishments of humankind. And it is impossible to understand those aspirations and accomplishments without understanding the religious roots from which they sprang" (p. 7).[12] Bennett disavows any interest in making America a Christian nation. Rather he wishes us to acknowledge that we are religious people and as such also the freest people on earth.

> A recent survey showed that while 76 percent of the British, 62 percent of the French, and 79 percent of the Japanese said they believed in God, fully 95 percent of Americans said they did. It is noteworthy that in each case, a similar percentage said they were willing to die for their countries. For the virtues that inspire patriotism—hard work, self-discipline, perseverance, industry, respect for family, for learning, and for country—are intimately linked with and strengthened by religious values. In short, the democratic ethic and the work ethic flourish in the context of the Judeo-Christian ethic from which they take their original shape and their continued vitality. The virtues of self-discipline, love of learning, and respect for family are by no means limited to the Judeo-Christian tradition that has given birth to our free political institutions; and it is the Judeo-Christian tradition that has shaped our national ideals. (p. 10)[13]

Evaluating the Alternatives

Perhaps it is very odd indeed to direct attention to Rorty and Bennett as alternatives for helping us understand our situation. Are we comparing apples and oranges? Rorty, after all, is one of America's most sophisticated philosophers and a representative of high academic culture. Bennett, while originally a philosopher, is now primarily a political actor concerned with addressing issues at their popular level. Moreover, one may well wonder if it is fair to present them as our only alternatives—surely we have other options for understanding the relation of religion and the state.

There are other options but I think juxtaposing Rorty and Bennett is illuminating for my thesis. For in spite of their deep differences, they share some fundamental judgments. It is useful, however, first to highlight their differences: the most obvious is that Rorty is from Bennett's perspective clearly the enemy. For Rorty wants to relegate religion (as well as all ultimate questions) to the private sphere in a manner that Bennett thinks is disastrous for our social order. Bennett, no doubt, would challenge Rorty to provide an account of how citizens will develop the virtues necessary to sustain Rorty's own preference for democracy.

Moreover, Rorty's disavowal of truth, the assertion of the political over the philosophical, leaves us devoid of any justification for preferring democracy, with its correlative commitment to freedom of religion, to that of totalitarianism. In Rorty's world we are simply left with the assumption that those who win the power game must be right. Fortunately for us, at least those of us who are at the top of the economic ladder in America, for the time being can enjoy the results of our forebearers' mistaken commitment to the religious and Enlightenment values that made the development of "free societies" possible.

Yet Rorty is not without resources for response. In particular he can charge Bennett with continuing to justify religious freedom in terms of the epistemological presuppositions of the Enlightenment that no longer can be sustained. For example, Bennett contends that "complete neutrality" must exist between religious beliefs and their public acknowledgment. Yet there exists no philosophical, much less political, position that can justify such a standpoint. Bennett wants to have his historical particular moralities—the "Judeo-Christian"— and the Enlightenment too.[14] But if Rorty is right you simply cannot have it both ways.

Moreover, I think there are strong indications that in this respect Rorty is right. For the religion that Bennett values is one that reinforces values that he has determined as good on grounds prior to the religion. Indeed, Bennett's very language of "religion" denotes an Enlightenment mentality that suggests the various historical faiths are but manifestations of a common phenomenon called "religion." The church may have freedom, but it does so only insofar as it can pass muster as a religion. One sometimes is almost led to believe that Protestant liberal theology was specifically developed to solve problems in American constitutional law and society.

The free exercise clause of the First Amendment has increasingly required a broad functional definition of religion, for otherwise government threatens to be-come an arbiter of orthodoxy.[15] Thus the courts can only inquire into the sincerity of a person's belief, not its truth or content. Thus the necessity of distinguishing between belief and practices that prove inconvenient to our society—for example, polygamy, frequent holy days requiring abstinence from work, the use of peyote, prohibitions on certain kinds of medical treatment—do not necessarily receive protection. These are the kinds of issues that help us see that former Secretary Bennett wants freedom of religion but one that has already been well domesticated by Enlightenment tolerance.

Bennett's attitude toward religion—namely, it should be taken seriously but not too seriously—is most decisively revealed by his interpretation of the First Amendment as exemplifying the commitment to the absolute value of freedom of conscience—that is the freedom to believe or not to believe. This is the value he suggests that American religions support as their fundamental commitment. Unfortunately, I do not doubt the descriptive accuracy of this judgment, but I have strong reservations about its normative status. Does Bennett really believe that thousands of Jews have died at the hands of Christian and pagan persecutors in order to make it possible for subsequent generations to have the freedom to believe or not? Jews rightly do not want their children to make up their own minds whether they should or should not believe; they expect them to be faithful Jews.[16]

Bennett senses that religion may be concerned with matters of truth, though I am puzzled by what he thinks he has gained by calling truth "absolute." Because truth can lead to intolerance, he thinks it must trim its sails to be part of the public discussion. Consensual values must be the standard rather than those that are "particularized." It is at this point that we see the fundamental agreement between Bennett and Rorty—both exclude the fanatic from political participation. The Loyolas and the Nietzsches must be excluded unless, of course, they are willing to admit as good liberals that their single-mindedness is but "their thing" and therefore arbitrary—certainly not something they would commend to anyone else.

In some ways, however, Rorty is more respectful of "the Mad" since he quite rightly sees he has no basis for saying they are irrational, but rather they simply cannot be seen "as fellow citizens of our constitutional democracy, people whose life-plans might, given ingenuity and good will, be fitted in with those of other citizens. They are not crazy because they have mistaken the ahistorical nature of human beings. They are crazy because the limits of sanity are set by what *we* can take seriously. This in turn is determined by our upbringing, our historical situation." Rorty does not deny, therefore, that such people have a right to exist; it is just such a pity they are so determined to torture their lives with such commitments when we live in a social order in which being a "light-minded aesthete" is such a pleasant and morally satisfying way of life—at least if you benefit from our economy.

It is not sufficient, however, for Bennett that fanatics be tolerated as long as they do no harm—they must be domesticated. They must cease being so single-minded and become "religious." For example, would Bennett be pleased if on just-war grounds the majority of Catholics in America became convinced they could not support our war strategy? Remember he took great pride in reciting the statistic that 95 percent of Americans said they believe in God and an equal number are willing to die (and one assumes kill) for the country. Fanaticism, that attitude that refused to subordinate one's religious convictions to the god of the country that protects our freedom of religion, cannot be tolerated if free societies are to survive. To be sure religion is important to train us in virtue, but such virtue must be armed if it is to be granted freedom as religion.[17]

But surely Bennett and Rorty are not the only spokesmen for how we should understand the place of religion in American public life. To be sure there are more insightful interpreters. To name but two, Robert Bellah and Richard John Neuhaus, though on opposite sides of the current political perspective, argue for the importance of religion in our public life not only to sustain our public ethos but to serve as a critical agent within our polity.[18] For example, Richard Neuhaus notes:

> To speak of American history of being religiously, even theologically, meaningful makes many of our contemporaries exceedingly nervous. This is especially true among those of us who embrace the proposition and the promise of liberal democracy. We are immediately reminded of talk about "manifest destiny," "the city upon the hill," and the "redeemer nation." All this, we have been miseducated to think, is the language of national hubris and chauvinism. Because we are so nervous about this language, we have left the task of articulating the religious meaning of America to those who do not understand the ambiguities of the American experience. The moral majoritarians do not hesitate to specify the place of America in God's cosmic purposes. Because we are so skittish about this subject, however, our mainstream culture is bereft of a critical patriotism that understands both vindication and judgment, both righteousness and guilt, both achievement and the way of pilgrims embarked upon an experiment of still uncertain results. Because of our nervousness, we have had for several decades now no public philosophy to guide our deliberations about what kind of people we are and are called to be.[19]

Such a critical spirit Neuhaus thinks most likely will come from the popular religious sentiments of the ordinary people of our society exactly because they have not been corrupted by the high culture represented by Rorty.[20]

Yet I am not convinced. In the first instance I am not convinced because I do not believe that Neuhaus can sustain his case empirically. William Bennett is the great theologian of American religion, not Richard Neuhaus. William Bennett, moreover, is a representative of the

kind of resurgent public religious consciousness that Neuhaus so urgently desires. Yet it must be asked where is the "critical patriotism" based on determinative theological convictions to be found in Bennett's position?
Against Neuhaus (and Bellah) we observe that the religion we have is one that has been domesticated on the presumption that only a domesticated religion is safe to be free in America. Rather than being a church that could be capable of keeping the state limited, Christianity in America became a "religion" in the service of a state which then promised it "freedom." For what *free* means is the right to entertain personally meaningful beliefs that have only the most indirect relation to the state. The state by definition is just since it provides for freedom of religion. The inability of Protestant churches in America to maintain any sense of authority over the lives of their members is one of the most compelling signs that freedom of religion has resulted in the corruption of Christians who now believe they have the right religiously "to make up their own minds."[21] There is every sign that this is now also happening among Roman Catholics. As a result, neither Protestants nor Catholics have the capacity to stand as disciplined people capable of challenging the state.

A Church Capable of Surviving "Freedom"

The other reason I am not convinced by Neuhaus's call to reclaim America's religious heritage is that I disagree with the theological presumptions implicit in that call—a strong overlap between church and world. Schooled on distinctions between state and society, American Christians have thought it possible to claim America as a unique social experiment in distinction to other states. As a result we have not faced the deep tension that must always be characteristic of church and world where "society" and the "state" are clearly understood to be "world."

For example, Max Stackhouse, in a lecture in the same series as that of former Secretary Bennett, rightly criticizes American Christianity for uncritically underwriting freedom as the dominant value for our social life. Against this he argues that for all the nobility of liberty it is not sufficient to secure itself. He contends all the great religions recognize this. Christians claim that Jesus offers them not only freedom from sin, despair, and death, but also calls them to discipleship.[22]

Stackhouse does not think religion necessarily will provide the new kind of public theology necessary to provide the basis for liberty, but he thinks theology might. By *theology* he means "the ongoing public discussion of how we can tell the difference between a decent and an indecent religion, between those which lead to chaos or totalitarianism and those that lead to human rights and pluralistic democracies. Theology is governed by the principles of truth and justice that reach across the faiths and across national, racial, sexual, and class boundaries. It has an epistemic and an ethical dimension. A public theology holds that ideas, especially when taken as the guide to piety among the people, make an enormous difference in real life. Nothing is so powerful as a good, tested, examined theory about what is ultimately true and just—godly."[23]

I have strong reservations about Stackhouse's understanding of a theology not determined by tradition, a theology that can transcend particularistic communities. My primary concern, however, with his position is that for all his talk of truth, he gives what, in effect, is a functionalistic account of religious convictions. Why should religious belief be judged by whether such belief is "decisive for the extension of human rights and the preservation of democratic institutions?"[24] What Christians believe about God may well be true even though it may not work out so well for theories of or practices of human rights. There are, after all, strong Christian presuppositions that at the very least relativize any claim that we might have to rights, if not denying them entirely.

Stackhouse is quite right that the issue is finally a question of truth. The question of the relation between church and state turns on the question of truth and how it is embodied in those two different forms of societal organization. Yet that is just the issue that has not been raised in the American context because we thought we had found a way to avoid questions of truth by substituting a political compromise, freedom of religion, for the nagging issue of how Christians should relate to the state. Moreover, the issue was even further confused by the Christian willingness to accept Enlightenment justification as the basis and rationale for freedom of religion in America. In the process Christians failed to notice that they undermined the very particularity of their convictions—the very convictions that are necessary for understanding why Christians believe the existence of the church is a necessary condition for knowing the truth of the way things are.

In that respect the kind of challenge presented by Rorty is salutary for Christians to recover why it is that the "truth" offered by the state is antithetical to the truth we find in the sacraments through which we are made part of God's redemption through Jesus of Nazareth. Rorty's "truth," for all its civility, is the truth that power and violence finally determine the cause to which we should be loyal. What is admirable about Rorty is his candor; he does not think there is any other alternative and says so openly. Moreover, he may well be right about the presuppositions of worldly political order. But

Christians do not believe that is our only alternative, not because we have a different account of the state, but because we have a different political order—the Kingdom of God. It is that which makes it impossible for the tension to be resolved between those who are loyal to God and those who are not.

The conflict I have tried to describe is not new. Listen to these words from John 18:33-38: "Pilate entered the headquarters again, summoned Jesus, and asked him, 'Are you the King of the Jews?' Jesus answered, 'Do you ask this on your own, or did others tell you about me?' Pilate replied, 'I am not a Jew, am I? Your own nation and the chief priests have handed you over to me. What have you done?' Jesus answered, 'My kingdom is not from this world. If my kingdom were from this world, my followers would be fighting to keep me from being handed over to the Jews. But as it is, my kingdom is not from here.' Pilate asked him, 'So you are a king?' Jesus answered, 'You say that I am a king. For this I was born, and for this I came into the world, to testify to the truth. Everyone who belongs to the truth listens to my voice.' Pilate asked him, 'What is truth?' "

Of course this text has been used to justify apolitical accounts of Jesus' ministry as well as the church—Jesus and the church deal with spiritual matters that do not have a direct effect on politics. Few well informed interpreters of the New Testament, however, would make that claim today. Jesus' ministry from first to last was political. His death was political. For Jesus died the death meant for Israel so that it might be possible for us to live faithful to God's way of dealing with the world—that is, through truth and not coercion.[25]

Jesus' disavowal of the kingship of this world does not mean that he is not king. Rather his dialogue with Pilate reveals that he is not the kind of king that Pilates are capable of recognizing. For Pilates are people who have disavowed truth, and in particular, a truth that comes in the form of a suffering servant. Even less likely is such a truth relevant to politics as Pilate understands the political. The fact that we are allegedly a democracy that respects freedom of religion has not changed that assumption. Rather the illusion has been created that we live in a noncoercive society because it is one where "the people" rule.[26] If the church challenged that assumption, then I think we would find that our society might well think us mad. In particular, I suspect Christians would find our society less than willing to acknowledge the church's freedom once the church makes clear that her freedom comes from faithfulness to God and as a result can never be given or taken away by a state.[27]

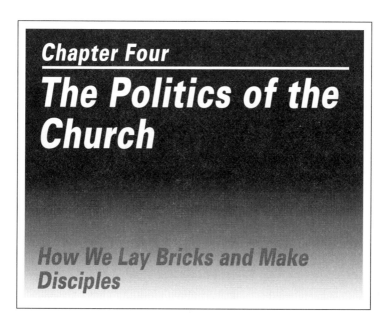

Chapter Four

The Politics of the Church

How We Lay Bricks and Make Disciples

The Statement of the Problem Is the Problem

The church seems caught in an irresolvable tension today. Insofar as we are able to maintain any presence in modern society we do so by being communities of care. Pastors become primarily people who care. Any attempt in such a context for the church to be a disciplined and disciplining community seems antithetical to being a community of care. As a result the care the church gives, while often quite impressive and compassionate, lacks the rationale to build the church as a community capable of standing against the powers we confront.

That the church has difficulty being a disciplined community, or even cannot conceive what it would mean to be a disciplined community, is not surprising given the church's social position in developed economies. The church exists in a buyer's or consumer's market, so any suggestion that in order to be a member of a church you must be transformed by opening your life to certain kinds of discipline is almost impossible to maintain. The called church has become the voluntary church, whose primary characteristic is that the congregation is friendly. Of course, that is a kind of discipline, because you cannot belong to the church unless you are friendly, but it's very unclear how such friendliness contributes to the growth of God's church meant to witness to the kingdom of God.

This attitude about the church was nicely illustrated by a letter in *The Circuit Rider* about The United Methodist Church. It read:

> United Methodism has been criticized roundly and at length for what it is not—not liturgical enough, not theological enough, not scriptural enough, not congregational enough, etc.
>
> I want to celebrate one ignored item not of United Methodism—namely, it is not harmful to religious people. In my work as a professor and parish minister, I have met all manner of people from other denominations whose minds and souls have been bent all out of shape by larger doses of rigor than many people can bear. Some folks have been given such high injections of some entities that their systems have developed a total immunity to the Christian religion.
>
> By contrast, even many of the people who leave United Methodism because of what it is not go on to lead happy and productive Christian lives as clergy and members of other denominations. Whatever they did not get in United Methodism, they did not get a permanent hatred of the Christian church or of its God.
>
> Wesley said it best. When asked what he intended to do with all those souls he was saving, he replied: "I would make them virtuous and happy, easy in themselves, and useful to others." Not a bad goal, Mr. Wesley! Not a bad record, United Methodism![1]

Such a letter no doubt describes not only United Methodism but the situation of many churches. As a result the church has increasingly found it difficult to maintain any kind of discipline that might make it identifiable as a distinct body of people with a mission to perform in the world. The church is very good at providing the kinds of services necessary to sustain people through the crises in their personal lives, but this simply reflects the fact that the church has become the privatized area of our culture. Of course this has had an effect on the very notion of the pastoral office because the ministers' authority is now primarily constituted by their ability to deliver pastoral services, rather than in liturgical leadership and the moral formation of the community.

The situation in which the church finds itself seems to make the activities of care and discipline incompatible. Care is identified with compassionate care of the individual and is now thought to be the first business of the church. Care requires understanding the particularities of the individual's situation so that the very idea of disciplining someone in a personal crisis is simply unthinkable. We seek to be understood and to understand—not to be judged.

In an attempt to respond to this set of circumstances, the primary strategy, at least for churches in the mainstream, has been to try to help people come to a better understanding of what it means to be Christian. Such a strategy assumes that what makes a Christian a Christian is holding certain beliefs that help us better understand the human condition, to make sense of our experience.[2] Of course no one denies that those beliefs may have behavioral implications, but the assumption is that the beliefs must be in place in order for the behavior to be authentic. In this respect the individualism of modernity can be seen in quite a positive light. For the very fact that people are now free from the necessity of believing as Christians means that if they so decide to identify with Christianity, they can do so voluntarily. When being Christian is construed in categories of self- understanding, with correlative senses of care, I fear that there is no way to recover a sense of the church as a community of discipline. Such an understanding of being Christian cannot help trying to cure our disease with more of the disease. The church cannot help become a life-style enclave and/or an umbrella institution where people are giving us the opportunity to associate with other people with their similar interests.[3] If we continue to follow the strategy that associates Christianity with certain beliefs or faith patterns, I cannot see how we will, in any fashion, avoid the trend so acutely described by Wuthnow in *The Restructuring of American Religion* of people being members of churches in order to be associated with people with similar interests that are not in any way shaped by Christian convictions.[4]

When Christianity is understood fundamentally as a belief system necessary for people to give meaning to their lives, we cannot but continue to reinforce the assumption that salvation is for the individual. It is one of the ironies of our time that many of those who are identified with urging Christians to engage in politics in the name of their Christian beliefs hold what are fundamentally individualistic accounts of Christian salvation. They assume that Christianity entails social engagement, but salvation was still identified with the individual coming to a better self-understanding through the world view offered by Christianity. The even greater irony is that the very form of society that was assumed to be the ideal for which Christians ought to work, namely a liberal democratic society, entailed the very presupposition that could only undercut any genuine conception of the social character of Christian salvation.[5]

In short, the great problem of modernity for the church is how we are to survive as disciplined communities in democratic societies. For the fundamental presumption behind democratic societies is that the consciousness of something called the *common citizen* is privileged no matter what kind of formation it may or may not have had.[6] It is that presumption that gives rise to the very idea of ethics as an identifiable discipline within the modern university curriculum. Both Kant and utilitarians assumed that the task of the ethicist was to explicate the presuppositions shared by anyone. Ethics is the attempt at the systemization of what we all perhaps only inchoately know or which we have perhaps failed to make sufficiently explicit.

Such a view of ethics can appear quite anticonventional, but even the anticonventional stance gains its power by appeal to what anyone would think upon reflection. This can be suitably illustrated in terms of the recent popular movie, *The Dead Poet's Society*. It is an entertaining, popular movie that appealed to our moral sensibilities. The movie depicts a young and creative teacher battling what appears to be the unthinking authoritarianism of the school in which he is teaching as well as his students', at first, uncomprehending resistance to his teaching method. The young teacher, whose subject is romantic poetry, which may or may not be all that important, takes as his primary pedagogical task to help his students think for themselves. Through great pedagogical sensitivity we watch him slowly awaken one student after another to the possibility of their own talents and potential. At the end, even though he has been fired by the school, we are thrilled as his students found ability to stand against authority, to think for themselves.

This movie seems to be a wonderful testimony to the independence of spirit that democracies putatively want to encourage. Yet I can think of no more conformist message in liberal societies than the idea that students should learn to think for themselves. What must be said is that most students in our society do not have minds well enough trained to be able to think—period. A central pedagogical task is to tell students that they do not yet have minds worth making up.[7] Thus training is so important, because training involves the formation of the self through submission to authority that will, if done well, provide people with the virtues necessary to be able to make reasoned judgment.

I cannot think of a more conformist and suicidal message in modernity than that we should encourage students to make up their own minds. That is simply to ensure that they will be good conformist consumers in a capitalist economy by assuming now that ideas are but another product that you get to choose on the basis of your arbitrary likes and dislikes. To encourage students to think for themselves is therefore a sure way to avoid any meaningful disagreement. That is the reason that I tell my students that my first object is to help them think just like me.[8]

The church's situation I think is not unlike the problems of what it means to be a teacher in a society shaped by an ethos that produces movies like *The Dead Poet's Society*. Determined by past presuppositions about the importance of commitment for the living of the Christian life, we have underwritten a voluntaristic conception of the Christian faith, which presupposes that one can become a Christian without training. The difficulty is that once such a position has been established, any alternative cannot help appearing as an authoritarian imposition.

In this respect it is interesting to note how we, that is those of us in mainstream traditions, tend to think about the loss of membership by mainstream churches and the growth of so-called conservative churches. Churches characterized by compassion and care no longer are able to sustain membership, particularly of our own children. Whereas conservative churches that make moral conformity and/or discipline their primary focus continue to grow. Those of us in liberal churches tend to explain this development by noting that people cannot stand freedom, and therefore, in a confusing world devoid of community, seek authority. Conservative churches are growing, but their growth is only a sign of pathology.

Yet this very analysis of "why conservative churches are growing" assumes the presumptions of liberal social theory and practice that I am suggesting is the source of our difficulty. The very way we have learned to state the problem is the problem. The very fact that we let the issue be framed by terms such as *individual* and *community, freedom* and *authority, care* versus *discipline,* is an indication of our loss of coherence and the survival of fragments necessary for Christians to make our disciplines the way we care.

For example, one of the great problems facing liberal and conservative churches alike is that their membership has been schooled on the distinction between public and private morality. Thus liberal and conservative alike assume that they have a right generally to do pretty much what they want, as long as what they do does not entail undue harm to others. The fact that such a distinction is incoherent even in the wider political society does little to help us challenge an even more problematic character in relationship to the church. Yet if salvation is genuinely social, then there can be no place for a distinction that invites us to assume, for example, that we have ownership over our bodies and possessions in a way that is not under the discipline of the whole church. For example, I was recently giving a lecture at a university that is identified with a very conservative Christian church. They were deeply concerned with the teaching of business ethics in their business school and had begun a lectureship to explore those issues. I was there giving a lecture called "Why Business Ethics Is a Bad Idea." I argued that business ethics was but a form of quandary ethics so characteristic of most so-called applied ethics. As a result, I suggested that business ethics could not help failing to raise the fundamental issues concerning why business was assumed to be a special area of moral analysis.

After I had finished a person who taught in their business school asked, "But what can the church do given this situation?" I suggested to her that if the church was going to begin seriously to reflect on these matters, it should start by requiring all those currently in the church, as well as anyone who wished to join the church, to declare what they earn in public. This suggestion was greeted with disbelief, for it was simply assumed that no one should be required to expose their income in public. After all, nothing is more private to us in our lives than what amount we earn. Insofar as that is the case, we see how far the church is incapable of being a disciplined community.

However, one cannot help feeling the agony behind the questioner's concern. For if the analysis I provided to this point is close to being right, then it seems we lack the conceptual resources to help us understand how the church can reclaim for itself what it means to be a community of care and discipline. Of course *conceptual resources* is far too weak a phrase, for if actual practices of care and discipline are absent, then our imaginations will be equally impoverished. What I propose, therefore, is to provide an account of what it means to learn a craft, to learn—for example—how to lay brick, in the hope that we may be able to claim forms of care and discipline unnoticed but nonetheless present in the church.

Teach People How to Lay a Brick

To help us get a better picture of what it means for the church to be a disciplined community, we ought to learn how to lay a brick. This discipline will help us think about what it means to be saved, what it means to be a Christian. To learn to lay brick, it is not sufficient for you to be told how to do it, but you must learn a multitude of skills that are coordinated into the activity of laying brick—that is why before you lay brick you must learn to mix the mortar, build scaffolds, joint, and so on. Moreover, it is not enough to be told how to hold a trowel, how to spread mortar, or how to frog the mortar, but in order to lay brick you must hour after hour, day after day, lay brick.

Of course, learning to lay brick involves not only learning myriad skills, but also a language that forms and is formed by those skills. Thus, for example, you have to become familiar with what a trowel is and how it is to be used, as well as mortar, which bricklayers usually call "mud." Thus "frogging mud" means creating a trench in the mortar so that when the brick is placed in the mortar, a vacuum is created that almost makes the brick lay itself. Such language is not just incidental to becoming a bricklayer but intrinsic to the practice. You cannot learn to lay brick without learning to talk "right."

The language embodies the history of the craft of bricklaying. So when you learn to be a bricklayer you are not learning a craft *de novo* but rather being initiated into a history. For example, bricks have different names—for example, klinkers—to denote different qualities that make a difference about how one lays them.[9] These differences are discovered often by apprentices being confronted with new challenges, making mistakes, and then being taught how to do it by the more experienced.

All of this indicates that to lay brick you must be initiated into the craft of bricklaying by a master craftsman. It is interesting in this respect to contrast this notion with modern democratic presuppositions. For as I noted above, the accounts of morality sponsored by democracy want to deny the necessity of a master. It is assumed we each in and of ourselves have all we need to be moral. No master is necessary for us to become moral, for being moral is a condition that does not require initiation or training. That is why I often suggest that the most determinative moral formation most people have in our society is when they learn to play baseball, basketball, quilt, cook, or learn to lay bricks. For such sports and crafts remain morally antidemocratic insofar as they require acknowledgment of authority based on a history of accomplishment.[10]

Of course, it is by no means clear how long we can rely on the existence of crafts for such moral formation. For example, bricklayers who are genuinely masters of their craft have become quite scarce. Those who remain command good money for their services. Moreover, the material necessary for laying brick has become increasingly expensive. It has therefore become the tendency of builders to try as much as possible to design around the necessity of using brick in building. As a result, we get ugly glass buildings.

The highly functional glass building that has become so prevalent is the architectural equivalent of our understanding of morality. Such buildings should be cheap, easily built, and efficient. They should be functional, which means they can have no purpose that might limit their multiple use. The more glass buildings we build, the fewer practitioners of crafts we have. The result is a self-fulfilling prophecy: the more buildings and/or morality we produce that eliminate the need for masters of crafts and/or morality, the less we are able to know that there is an alternative.

In his Gifford Lectures, *Three Rival Versions of Moral Inquiry: Encyclopedia, Genealogy and Tradition,* Alasdair MacIntyre develops an extensive account of the craftlike nature of morality. In contrast to modernity, MacIntyre argues that the moral good is not available to any intelligent person no matter what their point of view. Rather, in order to be moral, a person has to be made into a particular kind of person if he or she is to acquire knowledge about what is true and good. Therefore transformation is required if one is to be moral at all. In short, no account of the moral life is intelligible that does not involve some account of conversion. This is particularly true in our context, because to appreciate this point requires a conversion from our liberal convictions.

This transformation is like that of making oneself an apprentice to a master of a craft.[11] Through such an apprenticeship we seek to acquire the intelligence and virtues necessary to become skilled practitioners. Indeed it is crucial to understand that intelligence and virtues cannot be separated as they require one another. Classically this was embodied in the emphasis that the virtue of prudence cannot be acquired without the virtues of courage and temperance and courage and temperance requires prudence. The circular or interdependent character of the relationship between prudence and courage suggests why it is impossible to become good without a master. We only learn how to be courageous, and thus how to judge what we must do, through imitation.[12]

Apprentices have to learn two distinctions before they can learn anything else.

> The first is the distinction between what in particular situations it really is good to do and what only seems good to do to this particular apprentice, but is not in fact so. That is, the apprentice has to learn at first from his or her teachers and then his or her continuing self-education, how to identify mistakes made by him or herself in applying the acknowledged standard, the standard recognized to be the best available so far in the history of that particular craft. Secondly, the apprentice must learn the difference between what is good and what is best for them with their particular level of training and learning in this or that set of particular circumstances and what is the good or best thing to do unqualifiably. That is, the apprentice has to learn to distinguish between the kind of excellence with which both others and he or she can expect of him or herself here and there, and the ultimate excellence which furnishes both the apprentice and the master craftsperson with their telos.[13]

These distinctions are absolutely crucial if the teacher and apprentice are to be able to identify the defects and limitations of particular persons as they seek to achieve the telos of the craft. Habits of judgment and evaluation rooted in adequate and corrupt desires, taste, habits, and judgments must be transformed through being initiated into the craft. The apprentice must learn that there are some things that only the master can do, even though the apprentice might well accomplish what the master has done through luck. But luck or native talent is not sufficient to sustain the craft, so the apprentice must take the time to acquire the skills of judgment and accomplishment necessary for the achievement of the good.

So all crafts require that those who engage in the craft must come to terms with and make themselves adequate to the existence of some set of objects conceived to exist independent of their initial assumptions. Accordingly, there is a realist epistemological bias intrinsic to the crafts, but it is not the kind of correspondence theory that derives from the Enlightenment. The Enlightenment tried to show that the mind was immediately appropriate to a factual world without training. In contrast, our minds are adequate to that which we come to know only by being formed by the skills and practices of a tradition. Such training, of course, not only transforms us but transforms what it is that we think we need to know. That is why there can be no knowledge without appropriate authority.[14]

When the moral life is viewed through the analogy of the craft, we see why we need a teacher to actualize our potential. The teacher's authority must be accepted on the basis of a community of a craft, which embodies the intellectual and moral habits we must acquire and cultivate if we are to become effective and creative participants in the craft. Such standards can only be justified historically as they emerge from criticisms of their predecessors. That we hold a trowel this way or spread mortar on tile differently than on brick is justified from attempts to transcend or improve upon limitations of our predecessors.

Of course, the teachers themselves derive their authority from a conception of perfected work that serves as the telos of that craft. Therefore, often the best teachers in a craft do not necessarily produce the best work, but they help us understand what kind of work is best. What is actually produced as best judgments or actions or objects within crafts are judged so because they stand in some determinative relation to what the craft is about. What the craft is about is determined historically within the context of particularistic communities.

MacIntyre points out that this temporal character of a craft stands in sharp tension with modernity's understandings of morality and truth. For it is modernity's presumption that any moral conviction or truth must be timeless. In contrast, the particular movement of rationality in a craft is justified by the history of the craft so far. "To share in the rationality of a craft requires sharing in the contingencies of its history, understanding its story as one's own, and finding a place for oneself as a character in the enacted dramatic narrative, which is that story so far."[15]

A craft is never static. Thus masters are granted authority insofar as they exemplify in their work the best standards so far. What makes a master a master is that he or she knows how to go further, and especially how to direct others to go further, using what can be learned from tradition afforded by the past, so that he or she can move toward the telos of fully perfected works. The master knows how to link the past and the future, so that the telos of the craft becomes apparent in new and unexpected ways. Therefore, it is the ability to teach others how to learn this type of knowing these skills through which the power of the master within the community of the craft is legitimated as a rational authority.

For a craft to be in good condition, it has to be in a tradition in good order. To be initiated into craft is to be initiated into that tradition. But as MacIntyre points out, such an initiation always involves at least two, if not more, histories. I come to the craft qua family member, qua community identity, qua training in other crafts. In order for my commitment to this craft to be intelligible, it must be understood in relationship to a hierarchy of crafts within a good community.[16]

I am not suggesting that we ought to think about becoming moral as an analogy to learning how to be a bricklayer, potter, or teacher. Rather I am suggesting that learning to lay brick or play basketball constitutes contexts in which we receive our most decisive moral training. As I argued in the second chapter, it is only the prejudice of modernity that would create a realm of morality abstracted from determinative practices like bricklaying, quilting, or gardening.

Moreover, it is just such an abstraction that makes it so hard for us to rightly conceive of disciplined care. To be initiated into a craft by a master certainly requires discipline, but it is the nature of such discipline that it is hardly noticed as such. That does not mean we may not be asked at times to learn to do things that seem to have no point, but in the doing of them we discover the point. When a craft and a community are in good working order, discipline is quite literally a joy, as it provides one with power—and in particular a power for service—that is otherwise missing.

On Learning to Be a Disciple

But what does all this have to do with the church? First it reminds us that Christianity is not beliefs about God plus behavior. We are not Christians because of what we believe, but because we have been called to be disciples of Jesus. To become a disciple is not a matter of a new or changed self-understanding, but rather to become part of a different community with a different set of practices. For example, I am sometimes confronted by people who are not Christians but who say they want to know about Christianity. This is a particular occupational hazard for theologians around a university, because it is assumed that we are smart or at least have a Ph.D., so we must really know something about Christianity. After many years of vain attempts to "explain" God as trinity, I now say, "Well, to begin with we Christians have been taught to pray, 'Our Father, who art in heaven . . .' " I then suggest that a good place to begin to understand what we Christians are about is to join me in that prayer.

For to learn to pray is no easy matter but requires much training, not unlike learning to lay brick. It does no one any good to believe in God, at least the God we find in Jesus of Nazareth, if they have not learned to pray. To learn to pray means we must acquire humility not as something we try to do, but as commensurate with the practice of prayer. In short, we do not believe in God, become humble, and then learn to pray, but in learning to pray we humbly discover we cannot do other than believe in God.

But, of course, to learn to pray requires we learn to pray with other Christians. It means we must learn the disciplines necessary to worship God. Worship, at least for Christians, is the activity to which all our skills are ordered. That is why there can be no separation of Christian morality from Christian worship. As Christians, our worship is our morality for it is in worship we find ourselves engrafted into the story of God. It is in worship that we acquire the skills to acknowledge who we are—sinners.

This is but a reminder that we must be trained to be a sinner. To confess our sin, after all, is a theological and moral accomplishment. Perhaps nowhere is the contrast between the account of the Christian life I am trying to develop and most modern theology clearer than on this issue. In an odd manner Christian theologians in modernity, whether they are liberals or conservatives, have assumed that sin is a universal category available to anyone.[17] People might not believe in God, but they will confess their sin. As a result, sin becomes an unavoidable aspect of the human condition. This is odd for a people who have been taught that we must confess our sin by being trained by a community that has learned how to name those aspects of our lives that stand in the way of our being Jesus' disciples.

For example, as Christians we cannot learn to confess our sins unless we are forgiven. Indeed as has often been stressed, prior to forgiveness we cannot know we are sinners. For it is our tendency to want to be forgivers such that we remain basically in a power relation to those we have forgiven. But it is the great message of the gospel that we will only find our lives in that of Jesus to the extent that we are capable of accepting forgiveness. But accepting forgiveness does not come easily, because it puts us literally out of control.

In like manner we must learn to be a creature. To confess that we are finite is not equivalent to the recognition that we are creatures. For creaturehood draws on a determinative narrative of God as creator that requires more significant knowledge of our humanity than simply that we are finite. For both the notions of creature and sinner require that we find ourselves constituted by narratives that we did not create.

As I indicated earlier, that is to put us at deep odds with modernity. For the very notion that our lives can be recognized as lives only as we find ourselves constituted by more determinative narrative that has been given to us rather than created by us, is antithetical to the very spirit of modernity. But that is but an indication of why it is necessary that this narrative be carried by a body of people who have the skills to give them critical distance to those of the world.

In some ways all of this remains quite abstract because the notions of sinner and creature still sound more like self-understanding rather than characteristics of a craft. That is why we cannot learn to be a sinner separate from concrete acts of confession. Thus in the letter of James we are told, "Are any among you sick? They should call for the elders of the church and have them pray over them, anointing them with oil in the name of the Lord.The prayer of faith will save the sick, and the Lord will raise them up; and anyone who has committed sins will be forgiven. Therefore confess your sins to one another, and pray for one another, so that you may be healed. The prayer of the righteous is powerful and effective" (James 5:14-16). Such practice, I suspect, is no less important now as it was then. We cannot learn that we are sinners unless we are forced to confess our sins to other people in the church. Indeed it is not possible to learn to be a sinner without a confession and reconciliation. For it is one thing to confess our sin in general, but it is quite another to confess our sin to one in the church who we may well have wronged and to seek reconciliation. Without such confessions, however, I suspect we cannot be church at all.[18]

For example, when Bill Moyers did his public broadcast series on religion in America, the taping on fundamentalism was quite striking. He showed a fundamentalist pastor in Boston discussing a pastoral problem with one of his parishioners. The parishioner's wife had committed adultery and had confessed it to the church. After much searching and discussion, the church had received her back after appropriate penitential discipline. However, her husband was not ready to be so forgiving and did not wish to receive her back.

The fundamentalist pastor said, "You do not have the right to reject her, for as a member of our church you too must hold out the same forgiveness that we as a church hold out. Therefore I'm not asking you to take her back, I am telling you to take her back."

I anticipate that such an example strikes fear in most of our liberal hearts, but it is also a paradigmatic form of what I take forgiveness to be about. In Boston one with authority spoke to another on behalf of the central skills of the church that draw their intelligibility from the gospel. There we have an example of congregational care and discipline that joins together for the upbuilding of the Christian community.

Of course if the church lacks masters who have undergone the discipline of being forgiven, then indeed we cannot expect that such discipline will be intelligible. But I do not believe that we are so far gone to lack such masters. Indeed they are the ones who continue to carry the history to help us learn from our past so that our future will not be determined by the temptation to live unforgiven and thus unskillful lives.

Chapter Five

The Politics of Sex

How Marriage Is a Subversive Act

Sex and Politics

No area of our lives is more fraught with confusions, both conceptually and in practice, than in issues having to do with sex. It is not just what was thought unthinkable and even unmentionable a short time ago is now commonplace. Rather it is that we are unsure how to assess these changes and determine their significance for the Christian community. Christians seem a bit embarrassed by their past "sexual ethics" yet unable to say what in fact we are for.

One of my favorite examples of this awkward position was the report sponsored by the Catholic Theological Society of America called *Human Sexuality: New Directions in American Catholic Thought.*[1] They criticize the traditional formulation that "the primary purpose of marriage is the procreation and education of children. The secondary purpose is mutual support and a remedy for concupiscence" as too negative, legalistic, and act-oriented (p. 85). Such "criteria" needs to be broadened so that the purpose of sexuality is more properly understood to be what is "creative and integrative." Thus "wholesome human sexuality is that which fosters a creative growth toward integration. Destructive sexuality results in personal frustration and interpersonal alienation. In the light of this deeper insight into the meaning of human sexuality, it is our conviction that creativity and integration or, more precisely, creative growth toward integration 'better expresses the basic finality of sexuality' " (p. 86).

The revision is unclear whether or not these new criteria have the same implications as the old. At the very least, it would seem that some of the prohibitions of the past will need to be reconsidered. The authors of the report think this likely since the traditional Catholic insistence that linked marriage and sex will have to be rethought. As they put it, "over the last several decades, a more positive valuation of sexual intercourse has developed within Catholic theology, recognizing sexual relations as an experience and expression of love. No longer is intercourse viewed as excusable, only if procreative. At the same time, modern methods of contraception serve to mitigate the danger of bearing children out of wedlock. As a result, the traditional argument against premarital intercourse is no longer as convincing as it was in the past" (pp. 157-58). Nor, one must add, is the prohibition against adultery (pp. 148-49).

Whether premarital sex or adultery is inappropriate can only be determined, the report maintains, by further study. For the crucial question is whether there is "any empirical data available which might support a claim that certain sexual expressions always and everywhere are detrimental to the full development of the human personality. Is there any empirical evidence which would indicate, independent of cultural influences, some uses of sex are absolutely detrimental to the structures of truly human existence? In other words, are there any culture-free sexual prohibitions?" (pp. 55-56) Accordingly the report notes that empirical studies indicate a high incidence of "cheating" in marriage on the American scene, but as yet the evidence is inconclusive as to the effects of such behavior on individuals involved and their marriage.

However, in the absence of such data the report takes a cautious attitude. Thus "while remaining open to further evidence from the empirical sciences, we would urge the greatest caution in all such matters, lest they compromise the growth and integration so necessary in all human activity" (p. 149). One wonders what such "further evidence" might be and how it is to be obtained. Do Christians have an obligation to experiment sexually, so we can obtain better data about the "creative and integrative" potential of adultery?

As far as I can tell there is only one clear case that is clearly off limits given the criteria of "creative growth toward integration" and our lack of good data about the forms of sexuality that more nearly conform to that criteria—that is, bestiality. As they say, "where the individual prefers sexual relations with animals when heterosexual outlets are available, the condition is regarded as pathological. . . . There is no question but that this practice renders impossible the realization of the personal meaning of human sexuality. Persons so involved need to be gently led to a deeper understanding and appreciation of the full meaning and significance of human sexuality" (p. 23). Which seems to me to be a clear indication that this is a report written by urban dwellers that have very little appreciation of farm life.

I have called attention to this report only because it says so clearly what I take to be a widespread agreement, by Christians and non-Christians, about how best to think about sexual behavior. For it is assumed, insofar as one needs to think about sex at all in moral terms, that the primary issue is whether sexual expressions serve "wholesome interpersonal relations." Put in the most common way the only question is whether our sexual expressions are or are not expressions of love.

Now juxtapose this way of putting the issue to recent feminist concerns about sex. For example, Catherine MacKinnon, in a series of powerful essays, reminds us that sex is power. In particular, males have had the power to create the world that women inhabit sexually. Thus "femaleness means femininity, which means attractiveness to men, which means sexual attractiveness, which means sexual availability on male terms. What defines women as such is what turns men on. Good girls are 'attractive,' bad girls 'provocative.' Gender socialization is the process through which women come to identify themselves as sexual beings, as beings that exist for men. It is that process through which women internalize (make their own) a male image of their sexual identity as women. It is not just as women. It is not just an illusion."[2]

MacKinnon notes how many issues that seem sexual from the male standpoint have not properly been seen as defining a politics. Incest, for example, is seen as distinguishing a crime against the family from girlish seductiveness or fantasy. Sexual harassment was first seen as a nonissue, then became a problem for distinguishing personal relationships. Pornography has been considered a question of freedom to speak and depict the erotic as against the obscene or violent. Rape is a question of whether intercourse was provoked, mutually desired, or forced—was it sex or violence? MacKinnon argues that each of these ways of putting the issue privileges the male prerogative and yet fails to acknowledge the political coercion thereby legitimated. For instance

> women notice that sexual harassment looks a great deal like ordinary heterosexual initiation under conditions of gender inequality. Few women are in a position to refuse unwanted sexual initiatives. That consent rather than nonmutuality is the line between rape and intercourse further exposes the inequality in normal social expectations. If sex is ordinarily accepted as something men do to women, the better question would be whether consent is a meaningful concept. Penetration (also by a penis) is also substantially more central to both the legal definition of rape and the male definition of sexual intercourse than it is to women's sexual violation or sexual pleasure. Rape in marriage expresses the male sense of entitlement to access to women they annex; incest extends it. Although most women are raped by men they know, the closer the relation, the less women are allowed to claim it was rape. As women's experience blurs the lines between deviance and normalcy, it obliterates the distinction between abuses of women and the social definition of what a woman is.[3]

The first reaction I suspect most of us feel, as *most of us* means men, when confronted by a challenge like MacKinnon's is to take a defensive posture. Yet while one may disagree about some of her descriptions, I think she is right that the ethics of sex is from the beginning to end a question of power, dominance, and thus, politics. I do not mean to deny that sex obviously has to do with interpersonal relations—or as I would prefer, intimacy—but I am saying that the very assumption that sex and intimacy are interrelated reflects, as well as requires, a particular construction that is determined by the politics of a community.

The very idea that is reflected in the Catholic Theological Society report that sexual ethics can be determined by discerning the patterns of behavior that enhance human sexuality reflects a politics. From where did the assumption come that there is an isolated phenomenon called "human sexuality" that can be discussed separate from the ends and purposes of a community? Such an assumption derives from the presuppositions of political liberalism that assumes sex is fundamentally a private and personal matter—thereby the fundamental question becomes whether acts of sex are or are not fulfilling and noncoercive. Therefore the Christian tradition's presumption that we can only begin to think about these matters in terms of practices such as singleness and marriage cannot help being subversive to the politics of liberalism and the correlative state powers. Indeed, in a world in which we are taught that all human relations are contractual, what could be more offensive than a people who believe in life-long commitments?

Marriage and Morals

To develop the political character of sexual ethics, I offer an analysis of Bertrand Russell's famous book, *Marriage and Morals*.[4] Russell anticipated almost everything that has been said subsequently about the interpersonal context for sexual behavior. For example, the parallels between Russell's views and *Human Sexuality* are quite remarkable. Yet Russell, unlike the authors of *Human Sexuality,* faced the political implications of his position in a candid and admirable manner.

Contrary to the popular impression, Russell was not a libertine, nor did he defend a libertine ethic. As a proper

Englishman, Russell simply suggested that sex is generally a good thing, but it is important that it be handled decently. Indeed, he was against those who feel no moral barrier to sexual intercourse on any occasion because, he thought, such a view trivializes sex by dissociating "sex from serious emotion and from feelings of affection" (p. 127). Sex is a natural need like food and drink, but it certainly involves more than hunger, for no one, whether civilized or savage, is "satisfied by the bare sexual act" (p. 195). Indeed, sex is enormously enhanced by abstinence and is always better when it has "a large psychical element than when it is purely physical" (p. 7).

It may, therefore, seem odd to appeal to Russell in support of my argument, because it is his central contention that sexual activity should be determined primarily by romantic love, as it "is the source of the most intense delights that life has to offer. In the relations of a man and woman who love each other with passion and imagination and tenderness, there is something of inestimable value, to be ignorant of which is a great misfortune to any human being" (p. 74). Such love, moreover, cannot be limited to marriage since it can flourish only so long as it is free and spontaneous, as "it tends to be killed by the thought it is a duty" (p. 140).

Even though legitimate sexual activity cannot be limited to marriage, Russell thinks that under certain conditions marriage can be the "best and most important relation that can exist between two human beings" (p. 143). By marriage, Russell understands that relation between a man and a woman where children are present (p. 156). Children, rather than sexual intercourse, "are the true purpose of marriage, which should therefore be not regarded as consummated until such time as there is a prospect of children" (p. 166). As soon as children appear, love is no longer autonomous "but serves the biological purposes of the race," and thus the demands of passionate love may have to be at least partly overridden for a time. It is important to try to secure as little interference with love as is compatible with the interests of children, as it is good for children that their parents love each other (pp. 128-29).

However, according to Russell, if we ask what conditions seem, on the whole, to make for happiness in marriage, we are driven to the curious conclusion that the more "civilized people become the less capable they seem of lifelong happiness with one partner" (p. 135). For a marriage to work requires that there "be a feeling of complete equality of both sides; there must be no interference with mutual freedom; there must be the most complete physical and mental intimacy; and there must be a certain similarity in regard to standards of value" (p. 143). Russell thinks that it is possible to sustain such mutuality for a time, but finally such relations are doomed to be broken by the "anarchial" nature of love. This being the case, the only appropriate social response is divorce, as well as the legitimation of extramarital sexual intercourse.

Necessary Social Changes

It is to Russell's credit that he saw clearly that his views required far-reaching social and moral changes. He understood that marriage involves issues at the basis of any society and that changing them means changing a whole social order. At the very least, Russell thought that his view required the liberation of women from the double-standard sexual ethic (p. 88). However, even more important was Russell's realization that this new sexual ethic would also require a transformation of our language and passions. For the old sexual ethic continues to be reinforced as long as we insist on using unscientific language like *adultery* and *fornication*. If we are not to be carried away by emotion in discussing such issues, we must employ dull neutral phrases such as "extramarital sexual relations." To continue to use terminology such as *adultery* means we will remain captive to the superstitious morality associated with Christianity.

Russell is in no way recommending an ethic that ignores the importance of discipline and self-restraint. His problems with such categories is that they have been applied to the wrong concerns. It is not sexual expression that is to be restrained, but the "instinctive emotion" of jealousy that corrupts our relations with one another (p. 143). "The good life cannot be lived without self-control, but it is better to control a restrictive and hostile emotion such as jealousy, rather than a generous and expansive emotion such as love" (p. 239). Therefore Russell, unlike the authors of *Human Sexuality,* does not assume that empirical data could ever show that a particular form of sexual activity is good or bad for the development of personhood. For it is not a descriptive but a normative issue—namely, what should we be so that we can be morally enhanced by certain kinds of sexual activity? Russell and the Pope agree that the issue is not whether their sexual ethics may or may not be enhancing for people in themselves. Rather the question is what kind of people we ought to be to be capable of fulfilling the commitments for human flourishing. For Russell that means we must be people who are schooled out of jealousy; for the Pope it means we must be people who are capable of life-long fidelity.

Russell candidly admitted that if we allow his "new morality to take its course, it is bound to go further than it [has] done, and to raise difficulties hardly as yet appreciated" (p. 91). In particular he was disturbed by the fact that implicit in the new morality was the decay of the paternalistic family and fatherhood, which he thought meant the assumption of the father's duties by the state (p. 89). He believed that modern civilization was requiring that the state take over the father's role, and thus reducing the need for indubitable paternity (p. 9). Because the economic, protective, and educative functions of the family are increasingly being taken over by the state, families are relying more on the emotive function to sustain their existence. But Russell notes that the emotive function of the family will hardly be sufficient to sustain it as a viable institution.

His argument in this respect is quite similar to that of the conservative sociologist, Robert Nisbet. In his book *The Quest for Community* Nisbet observed that while the family continues to be celebrated from pulpit and rostrum as indispensable to the economy and the state, in point of fact it is indispensable to neither. Noting that people do not live together merely to be together but to do something together, Nisbet argues that without any concrete perceived functions it is unlikely the family can even continue to exert any strong psychological influence.[5] Alternatively, in the absence of any function, the family becomes psychologically too intense, for family members cannot allow themselves psychological distance from one another; otherwise they have no reason for being.

The State as Parent

Russell believes the loss of the family as a central social institution presents a problem, however, because the family's most important function is to preserve the habit of having children (p. 187). But since the father is redundant, women will have to share their children with the state. He thinks this may cause a problem in the "psychology and activities of men," for it will eliminate the only emotive function equal in importance to sexual love. As a result, sexual love itself might be trivialized, but more important, men's sense of history and tradition would be diminished. However, at the same time, men might become less prone to war and less acquisitive since they no longer have "their" family to protect or sustain.

However, the change in women's attitudes and practices will be equally profound, for there is no reason to think that with the increasing equality of women we can assume that women will "naturally" want to be mothers. As a result, in order to maintain a high civilization, it may increasingly become necessary to pay women "such sums for the production of children as to make them feel it worthwhile as a money-making career" (p. 216). Not all women will need to enter the "profession of having children," but at least some form of compensation will be needed to ensure that some women are willing to have children and some are willing to rear them.

Russell thinks that there are some distinct advantages in having the state as a father, since the arrangement improves both the general level of education and the level of health care. However, since he was not a "great admirer of the state," he also suggests that there are some distinct dangers in the substitution of the state for the father. For parents as a rule are fond of their children and do not regard them as material for political schemes. But the state cannot be expected to share this attitude.

As a result—and here it is worth quoting Russell at length:

So long as the world remains divided into competing militaristic states, the substitution of public bodies for parents in education means an intensification of what is called patriotism, i.e., a willingness to indulge in mutual extermination without a moment's hesitation, whenever the governments feel so inclined. Undoubtedly patriotism, so called, is the gravest danger to which civilization is at present exposed, and anything that increases its virulence is more to be dreaded than plague, pestilence, and famine. At present young people have a divided loyalty, on the one hand to their parents, on the other to the State. If it should happen that their sole loyalty was to the State, there is grave reason to fear that the world would become even more bloodthirsty than it is at present. I think, therefore, that so long as the problem of internationalism remains unsolved, the increasing share of the State in the education and care of children has dangers so grave as to outweigh its undoubted advantages. (pp. 218-19)

This view puts Russell in a peculiar position. For he has argued on interpersonal grounds for an ethics of sex that he assumes must render problematic the continued existence of the patriarchal family. Yet the eradication of such a family results in increasing the power of the state—the entity that Russell considers to be even more morally questionable than the old sex morality associated with Christianity. As a result he concludes that the full implementation of his sex ethic must await the institutionalization of a more complete internationalism that will qualify the power of nation-states to make war. Thus, he suggests that everywhere his sex ethic is taught there must be a corresponding inculcation of loyalty to the "international super-State." The problem, however, is that "the family is decaying fast, and internationalism is growing slowly. The situation, therefore, is one which justifies grave apprehensions. Nevertheless, it is not hopeless, since internationalism may grow more quickly in the future than it has done in the past" (pp. 219-20).

Thus, even though Russell begins with an interpersonal analysis of sexual ethics, it leads him to questions regarding the structure of nations and empires. Indeed, one has the impression that Russell was a bit surprised by his own conclusion, as it in effect suggests the need for a rewriting of his book. For to say that his sex ethic must still be compromised by commitment to the family, as long as we do not have an institutionalized international state, is a little like recommending partial pregnancy. His own argument adequately demonstrates that he cannot have it both ways, and yet he tries to do so.

Of course, one can argue that Russell's argument fails to demonstrate that the political questions are primary because his own analysis is flawed. For example, it is not clear that his "new sex ethic" necessarily leads to the destruction of the family and the heightening of the state's power. It is certainly a mistake for Russell to assume that only the "patriarchal family" is at issue, as there are certainly other ways of conceiving familial organization. But even assuming some other familial structure, Russell has still gotten the issue right: How should our lives be formed so that our lives sexually can give life rather than being used for destructive powers?

Marriage in the Christian Tradition

Put differently, the implication of Russell's argument, despite his own views to the contrary, is this: in order to talk sensibly about sex you must have available determinative practices that place such discussions in a purposive framework. Ironically, that is the point decisively rejected by the authors of *Human Sexuality* as being conservative and life-denying. It is not my intention to defend everything the Roman Catholic encyclical tradition has had to say about sex and marriage but rather to point out that that tradition, especially in *Arcanum Divinae Suprentiae* (1880), at least had the argument in the right ballpark—namely, that what one says about sex is correlative to one's understanding of the nature of the family and why the Church, not the state, claims for herself the primary jurisdiction over marriage. Thus Leo XIII claimed that "marriage is holy by its own power, in its own nature, and of itself, it ought not to be regulated and administered by the will of civil rulers, but by the divine authority of the Church, which alone in sacred matters professes the office of teaching."[6]

However, it may be felt that by introducing the concept of family and marriage I have in fact reinserted the interpersonal criterion into the discussion under a different guise. The interpersonal criterion certainly reflects the dominant understanding of marriage in our culture, but I am not accepting that meaning of marriage as my own. There is ample evidence to suggest that such an understanding is disastrous both personally and politically. When Christians assume that their task is to try to make such a view of marriage work, they take upon themselves a Sisyphean task.

We must understand that if Christians and non-Christians differ over marriage, that difference does not lie in their understanding of the quality of interpersonal relationships needed to enter or sustain a marriage, but rather in a disagreement about the nature of marriage and its place in the Christian and national community. Christians above all should note that there are no conceptual or institutional reasons that require love—at least, love understood as a psychological state of mutual good feeling—between the parties to exist in order for a marriage to be a marriage.

The requirement of love in marriage is not correlative to the intrinsic nature of marriage but is based on the admonition for Christians to love one another. We do not love because we are married, but because we are Christian. We may, however, learn what such love is like within the context of marriage. For the Christian tradition claims that marriage helps to support an inclusive community of love by grounding it in a pattern of faithfulness toward another. The love that is required in marriage functions politically by defining the nature of Christian social order into which children are welcomed and trained.

Therefore Christians do not believe marriage and the family exist for themselves, but rather serve the ends of the more determinative community called church. The assumption that the family is an end in itself can only make the family and marriage more personally destructive. When families exist for no reason other than their own existence, they become quasi-churches, which ask sacrifices far too great and for insufficient reasons. The risk of families that demand that we love one another can be taken only when there are sustaining communities with sufficient convictions that can provide means to form and limit the status of the family. If the family does stand as a necessary check on the state, it does so because it first has a place in an institution that more determinatively stands against the state—the church.

Christian Ambivalence Toward Marriage and the Family

The first enemy of the family is the church. Even Russell noticed that Christianity has had an ambivalent attitude toward the family which he wrongly attributed to the working out of the Christian emphasis on the individual.[7] In fact the ambivalence of the church toward marriage and family is grounded in the eschatological conviction that we live in the end times. The church as the community of that time is freed from the necessity of marriage. In other words, for Christians it is as good to be single as it is to be married.[8]

Though this emphasis on singleness has sometimes been interpreted as the result of a negative attitude toward sex, that is not its rationale. It cannot be denied, however, that when the eschatological context for the intelligibility of singleness is lost, corrupting alternative explanations are often difficult to resist. Yet it is not the threat of sex that makes Christians open to singleness, but rather singleness is that practice intrinsic to the church, so that we are reminded as a people we live by hope, not biology. Put simply, singleness reminds the church we grow not through biological ascription but through witness and hospitality to the stranger—who often turns out to be our biological child. As Christians we believe that every Christian in one generation might be called to singleness, yet God will create the church anew.

In an odd way there is a deep commonality between the church and liberalism, particularly in its economic form we call capitalism, concerning the family. For liberalism is also at war against the family insofar as familial ties might qualify our ability to shape our lives according to economic necessity—that is, the willingness to move to another economic function.[9] The church also attacks familial loyalties by reminding us that our true home is not the biological family but the church. Thus Christians are taught to love one another in the family while never forgetting that we can only love one another well if we, and our children, are prepared to die for the faith. We can never forget that Christians took their children with them to martyrdom—better to die than to be raised a pagan.

The difference between the church and liberal social orders' critical perspective toward the family is the narrative that shapes that perspective. The liberal assumes it is his or her task to make the family as much as possible a voluntary institution—I can choose who to marry and when—as well as whether to stay married. This is seen as part of the progressive story of freedom. The only difficulty is how to explain why I do or should feel obligation to parents I did not choose, and perhaps, even to my own children once it is clear they are not the ones I wanted.

In contrast, the story that forms the church's attitude toward the family is that we are not our own. We owe our lives to the gift of others. We are called not to be free but to be of service, which may take the form of singleness or marriage. The fact that we find ourselves tied to people we did not choose, who may or may not be our biological parents, is but a reminder that our lives are constituted by a narrative of creation and redemption that is not our own making.[10]

I realize this emphasis on singleness that I have highlighted will strike many as unusual. For it is surely an odd community that can risk giving singleness an equal status with marriage and the family. That the church can do so is only explicable on the grounds that the church is part of a history that the world cannot know apart from the baptism offered by the risen Christ. Singleness is the way of being Christian because we know we live by a hope in God's good rule through the church. Without that hope singleness cannot help becoming a way to protect ourselves from the reality of the other. In our culture, singleness too easily becomes the way we learn to name loneliness as independence and freedom. In contrast singleness in the church must become the occasion for friendship as we know we are linked by a communion that allows our differences to become the occasion for recognition of the other as other. If singleness should play the role I say, then Christians must surely be a people with a genius for friendship.[11]

How we live sexually cannot simply be oriented to what serves marriage and the family. Rather Christians must learn to think about our sexual lives as members of a community. We are called to be of service to one another as single and as married. This cannot simply be a matter of do's and don'ts, but rather hard won wisdom about how a community capable of standing against the powers of this age is called to live. Our sexual ethic can only be a correlative of this more determinative politics.

What Might a Christian Sexual Ethic Look Like?

Yet you are right to ask, "But what does that mean? You have to pay up sometime. What are you going to say about 'pre-marital' sex, about sex in 'meaningful relationship,' about homosexuality?" I am quite happy to declare myself on these matters, but such declarations unfortunately tend to undermine my argument. For it makes it appear that if we could just be more assured about the right or wrong, then our young, as well as ourselves, would not live in such a sexually anarchic manner.

I must admit, moreover, particularly when confronted by the kind of analysis of Catherine MacKinnon, I think a little rule morality might help. It seems to me good to teach young men and women who, like all of us, are captured by patterns of domination that the first word they must say is "no." Yet I fear such a "no" has little power in cultures when sex is the only game in town. How can we expect our young to relate to one another differently when sex has become the primary way they are given to discover what another person is like? To be sure lust may be a problem, particularly for the young, but I suspect loneliness and power over another are at least as important in our desire for another. Until we, young and adult alike, have our attention grasped by an adventure so true, compelling, and demanding we lose our sense of need, I think there is little any "ethic" can do.

But, of course, it is just such a narrative, such an adventure, I have tried to suggest the church is about. For we believe as Christians we have been invited to be part of that extraordinary adventure we call God's kingdom. That kingdom challenges the forms of domination we exercise over others that we all too willingly accept in the name of "relationships." Such a challenge can be issued because we have learned to subordinate all goods to God—including the good of our sex.

For if singleness embodies our hope as Christians, marriage and the family shapes our patience. Just as hope is not a virtue peculiar to the single, so hope is not restricted to the family. This is particularly the case once we recognize that everyone in the Christian community is called in quite different ways to the office of parenthood. Yet it is nonetheless significant in such a world in rebellion against its good creator, Christians are given the time to have and welcome children, not for the use of the state, but because we know that God rejoices in such life. To be a community capable of having and raising children, which in our society is relegated to the private realm, turns out to be for Christians our most decisive political practice.

Chapter Six

The Politics of Witness

How We Educate Christians in Liberal Societies

On the "Tonto" Principle

The story goes that one time the Lone Ranger and his faithful Indian sidekick, Tonto, found themselves surrounded by twenty-thousand Sioux. The Lone Ranger turned to Tonto and asked, "What do you think we ought to do, Tonto?" Tonto responded, "What do you mean by 'we,' white man?" An amusing story, but one whose implications are not easy for those of us schooled by Enlightenment presumptions to understand, much less act on. For the "Tonto" principle means that we cannot avoid asking Alasdair MacIntyre's questions, "Whose justice? Which rationality?"

For example, as representatives of cultures formed by the cosmopolitan outlook of modernity we simply assume that it is always possible to communicate with another linguistic community.[1] Whatever difficulties such communications may have can be overcome through education. Thus it is assumed that one language is always, in principle, translatable into another. While there is no doubt about the possibility of

133

translation of some sayings, this account of translation
assumes that there is something like English as such or
Hebrew as such or Latin as such, which can be translated
one into another. But as MacInytre argues, there are no
such languages but only "Latin-as-written-and-spoken-
in-the-Rome-of-Cicero and Irish-as-written-and-
spoken-in-sixteenth-century-Ulster. The boundaries of
a language are the boundaries of some linguistic
community which is also a social community."[2] Thus the
Irish "Doire Columcille" can never be translated into the
English "Londonderry" once it is recognized that even
names for persons and places are not only used *as*
identifications but *for* those who share the same beliefs
and presumptions about legitimate authority.[3] In fact,
"Doire Columcille" resides in a different narrative
tradition than "Londonderry."

MacIntyre reminds us that arguments concerning
commensurability and incommensurability have failed
to attend to the difference between language as such and
language in use.[4] To know the latter is to be part of
practices and habits that allow one to know how to go on
in a manner that is poetic. Thus, according to MacIntyre,
the young are initiated into such languages through
poetic expression. "It is in hearing and learning and later
in reading spoken and written poetic texts that the young
in the type of society with which we are concerned learn
the paradigmatic uses of key expressions at the same time
and inseparably from their learning the model of the
exemplifications of the virtues, the legitimating gene-
alogies of their community, and its key prescription.
Learning its language and being initiated into their
community's traditions is one and the same initiation."[5]

Yet modernity is characterized by the development of
late twentieth-century English, an internationalized
language, which has been developed so that it can

become potentially available to anyone and everyone, whatever their membership in any or no community.[6] This reinforces one of the defining beliefs of modernity—namely, that we are able to understand everything from human culture and history no matter how alien. That we might not be able to reach a common understanding with another is unthinkable. All we have is a problem of communication that another's learning of our language will surely solve.

The institution we use to achieve this kind of communication is the school. Of course, education is a much more general activity than what happens in our schools. Indeed, I suspect the most determinative education that we receive in modern societies is that received outside schools, whether they be public or private, secular or church-related. Yet schools are the places where we legitimate the assumptions that we basically share the same language, which makes communication possible between diverse and different peoples. This, we believe, is what makes a pluralist society possible.

Yet the Sioux will not go away. And the battle is being waged in the schools from the elementary grades through the university. Blacks, Native Americans, and women have challenged the alleged bias of the curriculum of our schools, both public and private. The depth of the challenge can be judged by the very terms used to describe the challengers—*blacks, Indians,* and *women.* Blacks do not wish to be known exclusively for their color; Native Americans remind us that there is no people called Indian, but rather they are Sioux, Blackfoot, Iroquois; and women often do not want to underwrite gender assumptions that go with the very designation, *woman.*

Moreover, they are quite right to be concerned about

such designations because much more is at stake than how a group is named. Putting the matter in those terms is still not strong enough, for what could be more important than how a people are named? If MacIntyre is right, a name is a shorthand for a story of who you are and what you care about. A name is power to determine memory for how the story continues to be told. The name, moreover, is a way to suggest who has the authority to tell the story. The names *Blacks, Indians,* and *women* too often sound like stories told by others, rather than how those people would tell their own stories.

I am aware that such claims often appear exaggerated, but I think it a mistake to dismiss them. For example, I think the most determinative moral training we provide in schools is the history told and/or presupposed not only in courses specifically in history, but throughout the curriculum. Through that history we often inscribe or reinforce ourselves and our students into traditions that are corrupt. Yet all this is done in the name of objectivity and rationality.

For example, no story grips the imagination of our educative practices more determinatively than the notion that "Columbus discovered America." Of course there can be disputes about whether Columbus was the first discoverer of the "new world," or whether he really discovered what we now call "America," but the main outline of that story is not questioned. It is the story that forms our educational system—privileging as it does the necessary background we call Europe, the Holy Roman Empire, the Roman Empire, Greece, the role of science, the great philosophers, and so on.

Yet Michael Shapiro, drawing on Tyvetan Todorov's book, *The Conquest of America,* observes that this story enshrined now in the language of objectivity effectively silences other voices. From Columbus we proceed to tell the story of the Spanish conquest by making the Spanish necessary actors in "our" narrative. Yet "in locating the Spanish rhetorically as discoverers of the 'New World' (and as 'conquerors,' which implies a different role in a narrative than 'slaughterers'), we reproduce the original Indians, not the Spanish as the Others, inasmuch as we trace our origins to that which we have called the European 'discovery' of the 'New World.' As Todorov remarks, 'We are all the direct descendants of Columbus, and it is with him that our genealogy begins, insofar as the word *beginning* has a meaning.' "[7]

Shapiro, I think, is right to draw our attention to the importance of accounts such as Todorov, because they illumine how "objective" accounts of "our" history can conceal the voice of the other. The Spanish, in discovering the "indian," in fact discovered themselves—just as whites "discover" blacks and Native Americans, and men "discover" women. Yet those very "discoveries" can mask a history of violence and terror that never ceases to be present in the ongoing descriptions—descriptions we need for our present understanding and action.

For example, Shapiro notes that from the time of the Spanish "discoverers," the Native American voice has not been able to challenge the practices which the nation of the new world entered into that produced what we call the "international system." He notes the first scripting of Guatemala into international speech by Pedro de Alvarado, Cortez's infamous captain, who described his subjugation of Guatemala in the following terms:

> After having sent my messengers to this country, informing them of how I was to come to conquer and pacify the provinces that might not be willing to place themselves under the dominions of His Majesty, I asked

them as his vassals (for as such they had offered themselves to your Grace) the favor and assistance of passage through their country; that by so doing, they would act as good and loyal vassals of His Majesty and that they would be greatly favored and supported in all justice by me and the Spaniards in my company; and if not, I threatened to make war on them as on traitors rising in rebellion against the service of our Lord the Emperor and that as such they would be treated, and that in addition to this, I would make slaves of all those who should be taken alive in the war.[8]

We—that is, those of us who inherit the "civilized social orders" made possible by the Pedro de Alvarados—recoil in horror at such brutality used against the Native Americans. Yet we must remember that the Pedro de Alvarados did not understand themselves to be brutal, but rather represented the drive toward the universal victory of Christianity. As Shapiro notes,

Christianity implanted in Spanish culture a social self-centeredness that equated everything connected with Spain and its Catholicism as natural, true, and right. Without getting into an extended analysis of this relationship between Christianity and ethnocentrism, it should suffice to cite as an example the Spanish *Requerimiento*, which was the injunction required by Spanish law, to be read to the Indians whenever Spaniards would first step on appropriated soil. The text gives a history of humanity centered on the appearance of Jesus Christ. Christ was the "master of the human lineage" who bestowed his power on Saint Peter, and in turn the pope, who, it seems, authorized the Spanish to take possession of the American continent. In addition to being informed, the Indians are given a choice: become Christians and vassals or "we shall forcibly enter your country . . . make war against you in all ways and manners that we can, and shall subject you to the yoke and obedience of the church." In this text, then, spiritual expansion and sovereign power are combined. More important, the universalistic notions of Christianity are incorporated into Spanish colonialist pretensions, producing a cultural intolerance toward things constituted as alien.[9]

Shapiro notes that the use of the *Requerimiento* certainly had its critics among the Spanish. For example, Bartoleme de las Casos strongly criticized Alvarado for "killing, ravaging, burning, robbing and destroying all the country wherever he came, under the above mentioned pretext [*Requerimiento*], that the Native Americans should subject themselves to such inhuman, unjust, and cruel men, in the name of the unknown King of Spain, of whom they had never heard and whom they considered to be much more unjust and cruel than his representatives."[10] Certainly Las Casos's position is more humane than Alvarado's, but Todorov argues that even this constitution of the Native Americans other has a subjugating effect. As Todorov points out, "Las Casos loves the Indians. And is a Christian. For him these two traits are linked: he loves the Native Americans precisely *because* he is a Christian, and his love *illustrates* his faith." Yet as Todorov further observes, La Casos's perception of the Indians was poor exactly because he was a Christian. Las Casos rejects violence but for him there is only one true religion, "And this 'truth' is not only personal [Las Casos does not consider religion true *for him*], but universal; it is valid for everyone, which is why he himself does not renounce the evangelizing project. Yet is there not already a violence in the conviction that one possess the truth oneself, whereas this is not the case for others, and that one must furthermore impose that truth on those others?"[11]

We recoil at this suggestion. If it is true, it seems we are simply silenced. Moreover, we fear its implications. For it seems to imply the very histories that we teach our children as Christians—the narratives acknowledged and unacknowledged—which we inhabit and pass on, are narratives that continue to legitimate the coercive imposition of the Christian story. It is no wonder that we seek to silence those whose very description—blacks, Indians, and women—challenges our claims to objectivity. The "Tonto" principle once acknowledged is difficult, indeed, to domesticate.

The Tonto Principle and Education

As I have already suggested, nowhere are these issues more acute and troubling than in our institutions of education. Of course the stories that form us, that we inhabit, are much more determinative in the practices of our culture than in education per se. Yet it is in our educational institutions that we reify those stories as "objective" and true. They become what anyone would believe if they just thought about it or were better "educated."

For example, think how the very idea of the "United States" is reified in the histories we teach in our schools. We assume they are innocent sets of objects that require no justification. They are simply part of the story. Yet as Michael Shapiro observes, when evoking the idea of the

"United States," for example, we could refer not to an administrative unit controlled by the federal government but rather to the process by which white Europeans have been consolidating control over the continental domain (now recognized as the United States) in a war with several indigenous ("Indian") nations. This grammar,

within which we could have the "United States" in a
different way—as violent process rather than as a static,
naturalized reality—would lead us to note that while the
armed hostilities have all but ceased, there remains a
system of economic exclusion, which has the effect of
maintaining a steady attrition rate among native Americans. The war goes on by other means, and the one-
sidedness of the battle is still in evidence. For example, in
the state of Utah, the life expectancy of the native
American is only half that of the European descendant.[12]

Yet in our public schools, especially in our public
schools, we tell the story of the United States as the story
of unity. It is a story, which may not as "history" be told as
a moral exercise, but it becomes all the more morally
powerful exactly because of its assumed "objectivity."
The extent of its power is nowhere better exhibited than
the inability of people, such as the Native Americans, to
tell their story in any way except as it fits into the larger
story of the United States. To fail to make their story "fit"
means they risk the description of being uneducated. It
sometimes seems the only option you have to resist
domination is by being a drunken Indian, a lazy black, or
an angry woman.

As Shapiro points out, however, there is little attempt
to resist the story we call the "United States" because it
contains the language necessary for us to do business. If
you employed the alternative understanding of United
States—as a violent process—you could not negotiate the
everyday. Instead dominant discourses about the United
States are accepted, which enable us, who seek to be good
citizens, political actors, and/or socially concerned, to be
concerned about "foreign policy" problems. For example, Shapiro calls our attention to *Time* magazine's article
on the death of thousands of workers at the Union

Carbide plant in Bhopal, India. The incident was represented with a photo of the victims with the large title that said "Environment." The obvious implication is that we should understand Bhopal as a pollution accident. That it was so treated may have to do with interdepartmental rivalries at *Time* and the environmental department may have not had a cover story for awhile.

These dominant presumptions are even carried over in the maps we use in our schools. In America the United States is always on the top half of the globe, because we are sure that north is up. We are equally sure that Australia is down, and it is much smaller than North America. The very nature of our maps, moreover, denotes our presumptions toward objectivity as they are meant to give us a complete picture of the "world." They are meant to impress by their close attention to detail. Our maps, those innocent objects in every first grade classroom, underwrite the Enlightenment story that we, that is we Americans, are rightly in control of the world because we can produce the "best" maps.[13]

Christians ironically have entered into this grand educational project in the name of objectivity, the quest for the universal, and most of all societal peace. For education, whether it be public or religious, in most liberal societies has had as its purpose, the suppression of minority voices in the interest of ironically fostering communication. It is true that in the past explicit Christian social orders suppressed dissenting voices, but it is even more the case today that the alleged pluralistic states of the present that profess to be guided by no visions of human nature or destiny are in fact, as Newbigin argues, guided by a very specific ideology of the Enlightenment.[14]

In the name of objectivity, which serves the politics of the liberal state, we have accepted the notion that the state can be neutral in religious matters. But as Newbigin observes, there is no way that students passing through schools and universities sponsored by the Enlightenment can avoid being shaped in certain directions. The very omission of religion from the curriculum of schools in the name of a fictional neutrality speaks loudly about what a society believes and wants its children to believe. Indeed Newbigin notes that for Muslims, who now constitute six percent of the English population and over eighty percent in some of the inner-city schools, the very idea of treating religion as a subject that can be put into a list alongside physics, history, and literature is itself an assault on the foundations of their belief.[15] Our neutrality about religion has been an attempt to suppress conflict in the name of peace but the result is the creation of people who think that all substantive convictions are a matter of opinion. They are violent only against those, like Muslims, who refuse to relegate to opinion those matters that matter.

The strategy of Christian education in such contexts, to supplement the secular subjects with courses in theology or to identify the religious dimension with concern for the "total student," has clearly failed. It is not sufficient to identify the religious with the "value" dimensions of knowledge, as that will only privilege the "factual."[16] Again, as Newbigin suggests, most modern accounts of the world exclude purpose as a factor in the ultimate constitution of things. "That the development of the individual person is governed by the program encoded in the DNA molecule is a fact every educated person is expected to know and accept. It will be part of the curriculum in the public school system. That every human being is made to glorify God and enjoy him forever is an opinion held by some people but not part of the public truth. Yet, if it is true, it is at least as important as anything else in the preparation of young people for their journey through life."[17] Moreover, I might add, that it cannot be excluded and in fact is required that any knowledge—including the knowledge of DNA—if it is truthful, must manifest the glory of God.

So we must ask why it has been blacks, Native Americans, and women, and not Christians, who have been challenging the curriculum of the so-called "public schools." Why have we left it to fundamentalists to challenge the reigning assumption that our world makes sense though all acknowledgment of the universe status as creature is excluded?[18] I suspect the answer is that nonfundamentalist Christians have feared appearing foolish in the eyes of the world, or less charitably, the eyes of nonfundamentalist Christians have in fact become the eyes of the world. As a result, we have failed to challenge those stories that legitimate the powers that rule us.

I suspect that we have been tempted in this direction because we have assumed that the universality of the Kingdom is now carried by the forms of knowledge sponsored by the Enlightenment. We think we are different from the Spanish, such as Alvarado, because we are not killing but only educating. After all, objectivity is the necessary standard for all right thinking people. Of course it is important to hear the voices of blacks, women, and perhaps even third world authors by introducing some works into our established canons, but such works must meet the standards of recognizable academic merit. In short, to be part of the conversation we have to agree to abide by the Enlightenment's *Requerimiento*.

Such a *Requerimiento* was nicely embodied in a recent advertisement that ran in the *New York Review of Books* (March 1, 1990) sponsored by an organization called the National Association of Scholars. The advertisement was titled, "Is the Curriculum Biased?" It began by summarizing the charge that the curricula of higher education are "Eurocentric" and patriarchal and the demand for the addition of more works by blacks, women and other minorities. The National Association of Scholars disputed these claims and demands by arguing:

> First, any work, whether formerly neglected or widely known, should be added, retained, or removed from the curriculum on the basis of its conformance to generally applicable intellectual and aesthetic standards. A sound curriculum cannot be built by replacing those standards with the principle of proportional representation of authors, classified ethnically, biologically, or geographically.
>
> Second, the idea that students will be discouraged by not encountering more works by members of their own race, sex, or ethnic group—even were it substantiated—would not justify adding inferior works. Such paternalism conveys a message opposite to the one desired.
>
> Third, other cultures, minority subcultures, and social problems have long been studied in the liberal arts curriculum in such established disciplines as history, literature, comparative religion, economics, political science, anthropology, and sociology. But more important, mere acquaintance with differences does not guarantee tolerance, an ideal Western in origin and fostered by knowledge of what is common to us all.
>
> Fourth, the idea that the traditional curriculum "excludes" the contributions of all but males of European descent is patently false. From their beginnings, Western art and science have drawn upon the achievements of non-Western societies and since have been absorbed and further enriched by peoples around the globe. That the liberal arts oppress minorities and women is yet more ludicrous. Even if the curriculum were confined to thought strictly European in origin, it would still present a rich variety of conflicting ideas, including the very

concepts of equality and freedom from oppression invoked by those who would reorient the curriculum.

Fifth, while diversity of background is valuable to the discussion of issues to which those differences are germane, objectivity is in general not enhanced but subverted by the idea that people of different sexes, races, or ethnic backgrounds necessarily see things differently. The assertion that cognition is determined by group membership is itself an example of stereotypic thinking which undermines the possibility of a true community of discourse.

Sixth, the study of the traditions and achievements of other nations and of ethnic subcultures is important and should be encouraged. But this must proceed in a manner that is intellectually honest and does not serve as a pretext for inserting polemics into the curriculum. Furthermore, "multicultural education" should not take place at the expense of studies that transcend cultural differences: the truth of mathematics, the sciences, history, and so on, are not different for people of different races, sexes, or cultures, and for that reason alone their study is liberating. Nor should we further attenuate the study of the traditions of the West. Not only is knowledge of those traditions essential for any evaluation of our own institutions, it is increasingly relevant to our understanding of other nations, which, in striking testament to the universality of the values they embody, are rapidly adapting Western practices to their own situations.

The National Association of Scholars is in favor of ethnic studies, the study of non-Western cultures, and the study of the special problems of women and minorities in our society, but it opposes subordinating entire humanities and social science curricula to such studies, and it views with alarm their growing politicization. Efforts purportedly made to introduce "other points of view" and "pluralism" often seem in fact designed to restrict attention to a narrow set of issues, tendentiously defined. An examination of many women's studies and minority studies courses and programs discloses little study of other cultures and much excoriation of our society for its alleged oppression of women, blacks, and others. The banner of "cultural diversity" is apparently being raised by some whose paramount interest actually lies in attacking the West and its institutions.[19]

I must admit when I first read this I thought someone had meant it as a satire. I simply did not believe that anyone could possibly believe that tolerance is an "ideal Western in origin" and was justified by knowledge common to us all. "Western in origin," I assumed, might give an indication that "common to us all" might be problematic. Of course the statement acknowledges the importance of conflicting ideas but fails to see that the very concepts of equality and freedom might not only be contested but might not and should not be acknowledged as goods. Moreover, the claim that there are studies which transcend cultural differences cannot help underwriting the story that underneath all our differences we all share the same story—namely through increasing enlightenment through education we will discover we all want the same thing.[20]

Christians have on the whole underwritten this story as our own. We allowed this story to become the "history" of our times. We have stood for allowing more voices to be part of the "history," but we have not conceived that the history itself might need to be challenged in the interests of the gospel. If we have to choose between those who represent the Enlightenment—those who MacIntyre calls the Encyclopedists—and those who deny rationality and morality altogether—those who MacIntyre calls the genealogist—most Christians think we must stand with those who still care about "truth" and morality and against those who "reduce" all conflicts to ones of power, who embrace "relativism" and threaten anarchy.[21]

What we must ask, however, is how Christians ever got ourselves in the position to believe we must make such a choice. The crucial question is how we can make the story we believe to be true not only compelling for us but for the whole world—a world caught between such unhappy alternative stories. In short, the challenge is how, as Christians, we can find a way to witness to the God of Abraham, Isaac, Jacob, and Jesus without that witness becoming an ideology for the powers that would subvert that witness. I think we can do that if we take seriously the very character required of us by the story that we believe to be the truth about our existence—that is, that we be witnesses.

On Witness and Education or Telling the Old, Old Story

I grew up with a gospel hymn called "I Love to Tell the Story." Its first stanza says:

> I love to the tell the story
> of unseen things above,
> of Jesus and his glory,
> of Jesus and his love.
> I love to tell the story,
> because I know 'tis true;
> it satisfies my longings
> as nothing else can do.
>
> I love to tell the story,
> 'twill be my theme in glory,
> to tell the old, old story.
> of Jesus and his love.

In spite of the lack of all theological, poetic, and musical merit, I am sure this old hymn has got the matter right. For it is only because we are storied as God's creatures that our only alternative is to be witnesses. Moreover, the only way we can educate is through witness.

What we must understand is that witness is necessary because we are so storied. If the gospel were a truth that could be known in general, then there would be no necessity to witness. All that would be necessary would be to confirm people in what they already know. If the gospel were about general human experience that is unavoidable, then there would be no necessity of being confronted by anyone as odd as a Christian. But because the story we tell of God is the story of the life and death of Jesus of Nazareth, then the only way to know that story is through witness.

The trick, of course, is how the necessity of witness, the oddness of witness can be recovered in a world that thinks it already knows what that story is about. The problem, as Lesslie Newbigin has recently stressed, is how Christians can learn to think of themselves as missionaries in a world that we have at least in part been responsible for making.[22] The problem is how we can critically appropriate those aspects of the societies in which we find ourselves, without remaining blinded to the destructive practices that are all the more powerful because they so often promise to serve good ends.

Such destructive practices are called powers in the New Testament. For the salvation wrought in Christ is about the conflict with and the conquest of these powers.

This point is so crucial for us it must be expanded: In the Epistles the narrative of Christ's conflict with and conquest of the powers is typically represented in summary, proclamatory form, as for example, in

Colossians 2:15: "He disarmed the principalities and powers and made a public example of them, triumphing over them in him." In the Gospels, however, these conflicts take the form of a story, indeed, they are *the* story, and the opponents are no longer called "the principalities and powers"; rather, they are the human overlords of state and temple, the Herods and Caiaphases, and Pilates, or they are the demonic forces that sponsor illness, madness, and temptation, namely the demons and Satan. These can be cast as actors in the drama—while abstractions such as "headship," "authority," and "power" cannot. Note further that the contra-power that Jesus (and through him, God's Spirit) mounts against these is nothing less than the whole course of his obedient life, with its successive moments of proclamation, healing, instruction, the gathering of a redemptive community, and costly submission to the way of the cross and its death and resurrection. Therefore it is at a decisive moment in *that* story that the Lucan Jesus says, "I saw Satan fall like lightning from heaven."(10:18)[23]

If we are to educate as Christians we cannot fail to introduce our children and one another to the gospel in a manner that helps us name those powers that would determine our lives. The only way to do that is by telling a counter story to the commonly accepted story of the United States and/or its correlative presumptions that underwrite the necessity of what we call the nation-state system. The moral and intellectual courage required for the task is great. Indeed, we cannot pretend to possess such courage on our own but we can only hope to fulfill that mission, as we would anticipate from the story itself, by being part of a community that can help sustain such witness.

As Christians this means that we cannot avoid coming

into conflict in school or state. Again, as Newbigin reminds us,

> Christians can never seek refuge in a ghetto where their faith is not proclaimed as public truth for all. They can never agree that there is one law for themselves and another for the world. They can never admit that there are areas of human life where the writ of Christ does not run. They can never accept that there are orders of creation or powers or dominions that exist otherwise than to serve Christ. Whatever the institutional relationship between the church and the state—and there are many possible relationships, no one of which is necessarily the right one for all times and places—the church can never cease to remind governments that they are under the rule of Christ and that he alone is the judge of all they do. The church can never accept the thesis that the central shrine of public life is empty, in other words, that there has been no public revelation before the eyes of all the world of the purpose for which all things and all peoples have been created, and which all governments must serve. It can never accept an ultimate pluralism as a creed even if it must—as of course it must—acknowledge plurality as a fact. In fact, it cannot accept the idea, so popular twenty years ago, of a secular society in which, on principle, there are no commonly acknowledged norms. We know now, I think, that the only possible product of that ideal is a pagan society.[24]

So what are we to do as Christians? Must we build separate schools? Perhaps. But such schools will be of no use if we continue to teach subjects as though what we taught is from anyone's point of view. Until the practice of what we teach reflects the witness we are called to make to the story of Christ, we will simply be wasting our effort. Such a witness can as easily happen at "secular" schools as religious ones. What is important is our willingness to take our story seriously for determining what we are to know as what and how we teach.

Are we not left, however, with the problem of Bartoleme de las Casos, the priest who criticized the use of the *Requerimiento* by Pedro de Alvarado, but who nonetheless was able to see the "Indians" as potential Christians? How can we be witnesses, how can we be educators, how can we communicate the gospel without explicitly or implicitly underwriting patterns of domination and violence antithetical to the Kingdom brought by Christ? If I have even been partly right, we can begin by acknowledging the gospel is a story, the story of Jesus. In the telling, or better in the embodiment of that story in worship, we believe is the power of God for our salvation. As Christians, therefore, we tell the story, not because we lack respect for those different from us. Rather, as Newbigin says,

> She tells it simply as one who has been chosen and called by God to be part of the company which is entrusted with the story. It is not her business to convert the others. She will indeed—out of love for them—long that they may come to share the joy that she knows and pray that they may indeed do so. But it is only the Holy Spirit of God who can so touch the hearts and consciences of the others that they are brought to accept the story as true and to put their trust in Jesus. This will always be a mysterious work of the Spirit, often in ways no third party will ever understand. The Christian will pray that it may be so, and she will seek faithfully both to tell the story—as part of a Christian congregation—so conduct her life as to embody the truth of the story. But she will not imagine that it is her responsibility to insure the other is persuaded. That is in God's hands.[25]

Appendix

What follows is a letter from a graduate student that I could not resist appending as the conclusion to this book. It is a reminder that the way of nonviolence is never easy and that our language can embody that violence in ways that we hardly knew.

September 27, 1990

Dear Professor Hauerwas:

I thought I'd drop you a note to comment on the Australian lecture you gave me. First of all, it may be that I have missed other places in your work where you carry the tone you have in this lecture, but it seems to me rather that I detect something new here. The bulk of the lecture seems to be an attempt to think through Christian complicity in the past and ongoing genocide of people like the Sioux, and an attempt to come to terms with how the universalism inherent in Christianity slips all too easily into the domination or the extermination of the other. These are precisely the concerns that have plagued me for years, and it is refreshing to see you confront them so thoughtfully.

As I was reading the lecture, I had in mind a friend of mine in Montana. He was raised a Methodist, then spent some time with fundamentalism, and then left the church and for the past 25 years has focused exclusively on the traditions of Indians, particularly those tribes which live close to Missoula, integrating himself as much as a white man can into these traditions. Two years ago, after semi-retirement from his previous teaching career, he taught for a year at the largest Indian High School in the country in Arizona, on the Navaho/Hopi reservations, where 95 percent of the 1200 students were Indian.

I think to some extent that this friend of mine carried a somewhat naive hope for the ability of Indiana traditions to speak to the world—until his year in Arizona. There, in the midst of an all Indian school, with Indian students, and Indian parents, and an Indian administration, my friend ran into a political situation that made his head spin. He had been invited there to implement a program whereby Indian traditions would be integrated into the curriculum. However, what he found was that the majority of the parents, teachers, and administrators did not want this program. First, there were the parents who believed their kids should be taught the old ways—and not by a white man. Then, there were the parents who thought their kids should be taught to survive in a white world and not be led astray by useless tradition. And then there were numerous mixtures of these sentiments in between. All these issues came to a head when my friend tried to begin a program whereby once a week a poem written by an Indian would be given to all the teachers, and they would then read it to and discuss it with their classes, so that the entire school would share for a day this one piece of Indian expression. All went well until the day that the poem the teachers found in their box was one called "Columbus Day." It read as follows:

In school I was taught the names
Columbus, Cortez, and Pizzaro and
A dozen other filthy murderers.
A bloodline all the way to General Miles,
Daniel Boone and General Eisenhower.

No one mentioned the names
of even a few of the victims
But don't you remember Chaske, whose spine
was crushed so quickly by Mr. Pizzaro's boot?
What words did he cry into the dust?

What was the familiar name of
that young girl who danced so gracefully
That everyone in the village sang with her—
Before Cortez' sword hacked off her arms
As she protested the burning of her sweetheart?

That young man's name was Many Deeds,
And he had been a leader of a band of fighters
Called the Redstick Hummingbirds, who slowed
The March of Cortez' army with only a few
Spears and stones which now lay still
In the mountains and remember.

Greenrock Woman was the name
Of that old lady who walked right up
And spat in Columbus' face. We
Must remember that, and remember
Laughing Otter the Taino, who tried to stop
Columbus and who was taken away as a slave.
We never saw him again.

In school I learned of heroic discoveries
Made by liars and crooks. The courage
Of millions of sweet and true people
was not commemorated.

Let us then declare a holiday
For ourselves, and make a parade that begins
With Columbus' victims and continues
Even to our grandchildren who will be named
In their honor.
Because isn't it true that even the summer
Grass here in this land whispers those names,
And every creek has accepted the responsibility
Of singing those names? And nothing can stop
The wind from howling those names around
The corners of the school.

Why else would the birds sing
So much sweeter here than in other lands?

Jimmie Durham, Cherokee

An immediate assembly of faculty was called, and my friend was grilled about what he thought he was doing by suggesting that this poem be read to the students. In the end, after a heated battle, the matter was settled in the following way.

Those who opposed the reading of the poem argued that such disturbing material should not be read to students who already lived such disturbing and damaged lives. In essence, they said they wanted to protect the innocence of the students, and to shield them from horrors which were so distant anyway. My friend and his few allies responded to this argument by suggesting that if it was the innocence of the students at stake, then perhaps the students should decide whether or not they wanted the poem to be read. After much protest, the faculty called three students into the meeting, read them the poem, and asked them what they thought. At which point a sixteen-year-old girl said something to this effect: "We know that our history is painful; we are not unaware of the horrors of the past; and what we expect of you as teachers is to teach us of this past, because regardless of the pain, it is the truth. And we expect to be taught the truth." Not another word sounded in the room; the meeting was adjourned; and the poem fell on the ears of 1,200 students. As my friend puts it, the student became the teacher, and even the most outspoken of those who did not approve of the poem had no response to what innocence had uttered. From there forward, my friend had to agree that he would discuss each poem with the faculty before it was distributed.

My friend came away from his experience at this school with a deep despair about the future of Indian traditions in America. If, at the largest all Indian school in the country, this sort of opposition to the traditions reigns, what hope is there? Indian schools seem only to legitimate the very history which continues to annihilate Indians (now via education). What a vicious circle it is.

This long digression is to say that it is with my friend and his experiences in mind that I read your lecture. On the one hand, he would be glad to see a Christian thinking so carefully about the Christian complicity in genocide. And I think there is much in your lecture that would be helpful to him, insofar as both Indians and Christians face the task of how not to be annihilated by the imperialism which is legitimated in the schools. And yet, he would, perhaps, be quite unsatisfied with the last two or three pages of your lecture. And, I must say, so am I, though probably for different reasons.

In the end, it seems maybe Gustafson's accusation of tribalism has a bit of truth to it. For I get the sense that beyond complicity, your presentation implies that Christians have also been victims of imperialism and that in that sense they stand as another tribe alongside the Sioux. Certainly this is right insofar as one follows the history of the martyrs. And yet, it seems to me there is a real danger in making it sound like Indians and Christians are in the same boat, when, from the view of the Indians you cannot get from beneath complicity so easily.

When quoting Todorov you say, "Yet is there not already a violence in the conviction that one possess the truth oneself, whereas this is not the case for others, and that one must furthermore impose that truth on others?" You then say, "We recoil at this suggestion. If it is true, we are simply silenced." Later on you say, "How can we be witnesses, how can we be educators, how can we communicate the Gospel without explicitly or implicitly underwriting patterns of domination and violence antithetical to the Kingdom brought by Christ?" No doubt you have identified the crucial questions, and you spend over twenty pages developing them in a most insightful way. But then, it seems to me, you do not do justice to the truth of the questions you have developed so carefully.

For all its merit, your solution of witnessing in the manner, I assume, of the Mennonites, does not engage the full weight of the questions you have raised—and for this reason: "Is there not already a violence implicit in the conviction that one possess the truth . . .?" It seems to me that Todorov would not be content with your move to witness because, though it answers the explicit problem of imposition, it does not address the first, and more important, part of his question. Reread the long quote from Newbigin and imagine that you are a Sioux: "As Newbigin reminds us, Christians can *never* seek refuge in a ghetto where their faith is not proclaimed as public *truth for all*. They can *never agree that there is* one law for themselves and *another* for the world. They can *never admit* that there are *areas of human life where the writ of Christ does not run*. They can *never accept* that there are *orders of creation or powers* or dominions that exist *otherwise* than to serve Christ. . . . The church can *never accept* the thesis . . . that there has been no public revelation before the eyes of all the world of the purpose for which *all things* and *all peoples* have been created. . . . We know now, I think, that the only possible product of that ideal is a *pagan* society."

This is incredibly violent and exclusionary language which has the rhetorical power of conveying that

Christians should *never accept* the *other* unless the other is one of the *all*. It labels and excludes the Sioux as the *pagans* (pejoratively construed) that they have always been.

Furthermore, when in the very end you turn to a notion of witness that is not concerned with the business of conversion, the language (again Newbigin's) cannot help sounding condescending. "She will indeed—out of love for them—long that they may come to share the joy that she knows and pray that it may indeed be so." It's as if you say, "Well, we know you are wrong, but don't worry because we'll pray for you, and with God's help you'll turn out all right."

Please forgive my tirade, and please don't mistake its origin. It is precisely because I think you have gotten so much right that I am so critical of where you end up. Your move to a sort of Mennonite witness which is a good one, but I think it is defeated by the violence of the Newbigin quote. As I understand Mennonite witness, silence may indeed play a role. You must depend on other people to be attracted to your life, not because of what you say, but because of what you do. And you can do so much without saying a word. Again, I don't think you do your own questions justice.

Of course, I am well aware that your move to witness is not meant to be a closure of the problem, and I do not have a better solution. But you might say more of how witness might be a sort of silence. Perhaps Christians should learn to shut up. I know this is no easy notion to work through, given the internal mechanisms which drive the Christian to proclaim the news, and yet it is precisely this proclamation which descends with such violence, at least when it is uttered in the tone of the Newbigin quote. I am also aware the Newbigin is discussing specifically the relationship to the state, where certainly Christians should not shut up, and yet the rhetoric of that passage is no invitation to the Sioux.

It seems that you are confronting in this lecture exactly

what I have called "humility in tension with truth."
Working with Nietzsche's notion of truth, Gilles Deleuze
says this: "The true world implies a 'truthful man,' a man
who wants the truth, but such a man has strange motives,
as if he were hiding another man in him. . . . Othello
wants the truth, but out of jealousy, or worse, out of
revenge for being black. . . . The truthful man in the end
wants nothing other than to judge life; he holds up a
superior value, the good, in the name of which he will be
able to judge, he is craving to judge, he sees in life an evil,
a fault which is to be atoned for: the moral origin of the
notion of truth. In the Nietzschean fashion, [we must
battle] against the system of judgment: there is no value
superior to life, life is not to be judged or justified, it is
innocent. . . " Now certainly much of this Nietzschean
analysis needs to be questioned, and yet I wonder if
perhaps Deleuze is not on to something here.

"Such a man has strange motives . . .": I am reminded
of the fixation upon personal identity which we find in
MacIntyre, and of his whole notion of the narrative quest
by which we seek to render our lives intelligible, that is,
truthful. Deleuze makes the point that it is precisely this
search for identity and truth via narrative that has
questionable motives because one is always led to judge;
and in the end, in order to acquire the identity MacIntyre
seeks, I am forced to judge in such a way that I cannot
help but lie. Quoting Nietzsche, "The truthful man ends
up realizing that he has never stopped lying." This seems
right to me. For indeed it takes an incredible amount of
deception to keep this self going every day. So much is
excluded from the continuity of narrative. And I wonder
of the motives which move so many of us to insist upon
identity.

Deleuze goes on to say that to do away with narrative
and the truth is not to do away with story telling.
Obviously, this would seem a problem. What the hell is a
non-narrative story? And yet, it may be that by at least
trying to think what this might be, one can move away

from violence inherent in MacIntyre's position, the violence that continues to kill the Sioux.

I have not thought any of this through, and am just throwing it out, but this is one of the things I find helpful in Deleuze. For one way or another, what needs to occur is a move away from (or perhaps into and through) this tension which you identify so astutely in your lecture, and which is certainly bound to the notions of narrative and truth. And your task is much more difficult because you are a pacifist. MacIntyre and Fish and so many others can stop where they do because they don't mind the killing, but you can't stop there, and I would like to think that I can't either.

I hope that you find at least some of my comments constructive.

Peace,
David Toole

Notes

Introduction

1. Alasdair MacIntyre, *Three Rival Versions of Moral Inquiry: Encyclopedia, Genealogy and Tradition* (Notre Dame: University of Notre Dame Press, 1990), p. 220. MacIntyre notes that Adam Gifford wrote in his will, "I wish the lectures to treat their subject as a strictly natural science. . . . I wish it to be considered just as astronomy or chemistry is" (p. 9).

2. For two very interesting accounts of what it means to be Australian, see Mal Garvin, *Us Aussies: The Fascinating History They Didn't Tell Us at School* (Victoria: Hayzon, 1987) and William Lawton, *Being Christian, Being Australian: Contemporary Christianity Down Under* (Homebush West, New South Wales: Lancer Books, 1988). For an absolutely horrific tale of the early history of Australia, see Robert Hughes, *Fatal Shore* (New York: Vintage, 1988).

3. I have tried both in *Christian Existence Today: Essays on Church, World, and Living in Between* (Durham, N.C.: Labyrinth Press, 1988) as well as *Resident Aliens: Life in a Christian Colony* with William Willimon (Nashville: Abingdon Press, 1989) to meet this often-made charge.

4. Michel de Certeau, *The Practice of Everyday Life*, translated by Stephen Rendall (Berkeley: University of California Press, 1988), pp. 35-36.

5. By *panoptic*, de Certeau is obviously appealing to Michel Foucault's *Discipline and Punish: The Birth of the Prison*, translated by Allen Sheridan (New York: Vintage Books, 1979). Many will see the influence of Foucault throughout this book. It is certainly there but I have not engaged in extensive conversation with Foucault, though I have been deeply influenced by his account of surveillance.

6. De Certeau, *The Practice of Everyday Life*, p. 36. As Foucault says, "It is often said that the model of society that has individuals as its constituent elements is barred from the abstract juridical forms of contract and exchange. Mercantile society, according to this view, is represented as a contractual association of isolated judicial subjects. Perhaps. Indeed, the political theory of the 17th and 18th centuries often seem to follow this schema. But it should not be forgotten that there existed at the same period a technique for constituting individuals as a correlative element of power and knowledge. The individual is no doubt the fictitious Adam of an 'ideological' representation of society; but he is also a reality fabricated by this specific technology of power that I have called 'discipline.' We must cease once and for all to describe the effects of power in negative terms: it 'excludes,' it 'represses,' it 'censors,' it 'abstracts,' it 'masks,' it 'conceals.' In fact power produces; it produces reality; it produces domains of the objects and rituals of truth. The individual and the knowledge that may be gained of him belonged to this production" (p. 194). That is why, of course, that Foucault is so powerful in his presentation of Bentham's account of the prison as a panopticon since Bentham at once was able to show how power is at once visible and unverifiable. The panopticon thus becomes the image for liberal societies as we now discipline ourselves, and those disciplines often take the form of sciences, without thinking. In fact, we are being governed by anyone other than our own wants.

7. Ibid., pp. 36-37.

8. For a wonderfully candid account of the relationship between Christianity and Western civilization, see Wolfhart Pannenberg and Richard John Neuhaus, "The Christian West?" in *First Things,* 7 (November, 1990), pp. 24-31. Certainly neither Pannenberg nor Neuhaus gives an uncritical account of the relationship between Christianity and Western civilization, yet they clearly want to presume that Christians have a stake in the preservation of Western accomplishments in a way that is different from other cultures. Of course, one of the problematic aspects of such an account is the presumption that there is something called the West.

9. John Milbank, *Theology and Social Theory: Beyond Secular Reason* (Cambridge: Basil Blackwell, 1991), pp. 391-92.

1. The Politics of Salvation

1. Those familiar with the work of John Howard Yoder will recognize his influence, and particularly his *The Politics of Jesus* (Grand Rapids: Eerdmans, 1972), for this essay and book.

2. George Lindbeck, *The Nature of Doctrine* (Philadelphia: Westminster Press, 1984), p. 134.

3. See, for example, Vaclav Havel, *Living in Truth* (London: Faber and Faber, 1986) and in particular his essay "The Power of the Powerless," pp. 36-122. I am not suggesting that Havel identifies with Christianity, though he clearly is sympathetic to Christian convictions. For example, he notes that many of the challenges confronting people in these totalitarian societies are not different than in democratic societies. "There is no real evidence that Western democracy, that is, democracy of the traditional parliamentary type, can offer solutions that are any more profound. It may even be said that the more room there is in the Western democracies (compared to our world) for the genuine aim of life, the better the crisis is hidden from people and the more deeply do they become immersed in it. It would appear that the traditional parliamentary democracies can offer no fundamental opposition to the automatism of technological civilization and the industrial-consumer society, for they, too, are being dragged helplessly along by it. People are manipulated in ways that are infinitely more subtle and refined than the brutal methods used in the post-totalitarian societies. But this static complex of rigid, conceptual sloppy and political pragmatic mars political parties run by professional apparatuses and releasing the citizens from all forms of concrete and personal responsibility; and those complex focuses of capital accumulation engaged in secret manipulations and expansion; the omnipresent dictatorship of consumption, production, advertising, commerce, consumer culture, and all that flood of information: all of it, so often analyzed and described, can only with great difficulty be imagined as the source of humanity's rediscovery of itself. In a democracy, human beings may enjoy many personal freedoms and securities that are unknown to us, but in the end they do them no good, for they too are ultimate victims of the same automatism, and are incapable of defending their concerns about their own identity or preventing their superficialization or transcending concerns about their own personal survival to become proud and responsible members of the *polis,* making a genuine contribution to the creation of its destiny." pp. 115-117.

4. Alasdair MacIntyre, *The Religious Significance of Atheism* (New York: Columbia University Press, 1966), p. 24.

5. In particular, see Havel's discussion of truth in terms of whether a greengrocer should display in his window the slogan, "Workers of the world, unite." *Living in Truth,* pp. 50-57.

6. Charles Taylor, *Sources of the Self: The Making of the Modern Identity* (Cambridge: Harvard University Press, 1989), p. 312.

7. Ibid., pp. 312-13. Taylor notes that crucial to the development of Victorian unbelief was the development of an "ethics of unbelief"—for example, one ought not to believe what one has insufficient evidence. Two ideals gave force to this principle: (1) that we have an obligation to make up our own minds on the evidence without appeal to authority; and (2) a kind of heroism of unbelief based on the knowledge that one has confronted the truth of things no matter how bleak. Obviously these attitudes are still present among some. Equally important for the development of the culture of unbelief, according to Taylor, was the turn from religion to science,

which "betokened a greater purity of spirit and greater manliness but also aligned them with the demands of human progress and welfare. Indeed, the courage to face the unhallowed universe could be thought of as a sacrifice which agnostics were willing to make for human betterment. In the words of an American unbeliever, their 'grand philosophy' taught them to lose sight of ourselves and our burdens in the onward march of the human race. And indeed, as with Bentham and the unbelieving Enlightenment, many cherished the notion that facing the Godless universe liberated reserves of benevolence in us. In the words of another American, 'the moment that one loses confidence in God or immortality in the universe,' one becomes 'more self-reliant, more courageous, and the more solicitous to aid where only human aid is possible.'" pp. 404-5. One of the ironies of our times is this attitude has been accepted by Christians who fail to see that the ideals they accept in the name of a better society, such as the elimination of suffering, are implicitly atheistic. That is the subtext of my book *Naming the Silences: God, Medicine and the Problem of Suffering* (Grand Rapids: Eerdmans, 1990).

8. Less I be misunderstood, let me say that I have no wish to return to a "golden age" in which Christians ruled, and I do not harbor a desire for a "Christian culture." I am not opposed to nostalgia as perhaps a necessary stage in any fundamental social criticism, but I certainly do not long for a time when something called "Christianity" had hegemonic culture and political power. Indeed it is my presumption that when such hegemony has existed the possibility of the church to lead the faithful is decisively compromised. At the same time I do not seek to make a virtue out of minority status per se. Being out of power or oppressed can be an occasion for corruption as much as being in power. As I shall suggest, the question for Christians is not whether we rule, but how. Our difficulty has been the confusion that the rule of Christ must take the form of domination promised by Caesar.

9. Taylor, *Sources of the Self*, p. 411.

10. Jeffrey Stout, *Ethics After Babel: The Languages of Morals and Their Discontents* (Boston: Beacon Press, 1988), p. 161. For a fuller discussion of Stout's nuanced position see my and Phil Kenneson's article, "Flight From Foundationalism, Or, Things Aren't as Bad as They Seem," *Soundings*, 71, 4 (Winter 1988), pp. 683-99.

11. George Will, "Scalia Missed Point But Made Right Argument on Separation of Religion," *Durham Morning Herald*, Sunday, April 22, 1990, section F.

12. Reinhold Niebuhr was the determinative voice that made love and justice the primary categories for Christian ethics. It was also Niebuhr's influence that made questions of the relation of freedom and equality to be the issue for any display of justice. Of course many have critiqued Niebuhr's understanding of the relationship between love and justice, but those critiques continue to presuppose that love and justice should be the primary terms for any Christian ethic. To his credit, Niebuhr understood concentration on love and justice was necessary once Jesus was rendered secondary for our social ethic. For Niebuhr's reflections on these matters see his *The Nature and Destiny of Man*, vol. 2 (New York: Charles Scribner's Sons, 1949), pp. 244-86.

13. Richard Rorty, *Contingency, Irony, and Solidarity* (Cambridge: Cambridge University Press, 1989), p. 8.

14. Ibid., pp. 51-52. For a defense of Rorty, see Stout, *Ethics After Babel*, pp. 246-55. Stout, I think, rightly suggests that Rorty need not be read as a defender of nihilistic decadence nor of emotivism, but then it is not clear what Rorty wants. For a critique of Rorty, see Ian Shapiro, *Political Criticism* (Berkeley: University of California Press, 1990), pp. 19-54. Shapiro points out that Rorty assumes that the basic relevant moral community is the national community, which I take to be a much deeper problem than either Rorty's alleged nihilism or relativism.

15. Anthony Giddens, *The Nation-State and Violence* (Berkeley: University of California Press, 1987), pp. 83-121.

16. Ibid., p. 121.

17. Oliver O'Donovan, "The Loss of a Sense of Place," *Irish Theological Quarterly,* 55 (1989), pp. 40-41. George Grant in his luminous book *English Speaking Justice* (Notre Dame: University of Notre Dame Press, 1985), states that liberalism lacks the ability to account for borders. That is why it is necessarily imperialist in its conception. As he says, "Western principles of right in claiming universality became at one and the same time the basis for anti-imperialism both at home and abroad, yet also a justification for Western expansion as the bringing of Enlightenment into 'backward' parts of the world. . . . The dilemma became increasingly obvious; insofar as modern liberals put their trust in the development of commerce and technology, they were inevitably identifying themselves with the spread of imperialism; insofar as liberalism became explicitly a universal doctrine of human rights, the liberals had to become critics of their imperialism." pp. 93-94. See also Alasdair MacIntyre, "Is Patriotism a Virtue?" (Lawrence: University of Kansas' Department of Philosophy, 1984), pp. 3-20. MacIntyre argues that most liberal accounts of the nation-state make patriotism irrational since the very terms of the justification of the community are meant to deny that the goods we enjoy are particular to this land and history. For an attempt to give a more positive account of patriotism within a critical liberalism, see Charles Taylor's "Cross-Purposes: The Liberal-Communitarian Debate," in *Liberalism and the Moral Life,* edited by Nancy Rosenblum (Cambridge: Harvard University Press, 1989), pp. 159-82.

    Daniel Kemmis has made these issues concrete in his wonderful book *Community and the Politics of Place* (Norman: University of Oklahoma Press, 1990). "The kinds of values which might form the basics for a genuinely public life, then, arise out of a context which is concrete in at least two ways. It is concrete in the actual things or events—the barns, the barn dance—which the practices of cooperation produce. But it is also concrete in the actual, specific places within which those practices and that cooperation take place. Clearly, the practices which shaped the behavior and the character of frontier families did not appear out of thin air; they grew out of the one thing those people had most fundamentally in common: the effort to survive comes to rely upon shared and repeated practices like barn raising, survival itself is transformed; it becomes inhabitation. To *inhabit* a place is to dwell there in a practical way, in a way which relies upon certain regular, trusted habits of behavior." p. 79.

18. In her contentious review of MacIntyre's *Whose Justice? Which Rationality?*, Martha Nussbaum makes the interesting point that MacIntyre's preference for particularistic traditions, thus his criticism of England for attempting to influence the local traditions of Scotland, is curiously at odds with his Augustinian form of Christianity. For as she notes, "No moral system has exterminated local traditions more relentlessly and more successfully than Christianity, especially in its Roman Catholic version. And yet, even while continuing to defend the integrity and authority of local traditions, MacIntyre gives his allegiance to Catholic Christianity." "Recoiling from Reason," *New York Review of Books* 36, (December 7, 1989), p. 38. There is no question that Nussbaum has put her finger on an extraordinarily important issue, not only for MacIntyre, but also for the position I am trying to develop in this book. What must be said is that the issue is finally not a question of universality versus particularism, as that is exactly the way the issue would be put from a liberal perspective. Rather the question is how the church's practices will act as a critic as well as be enriched by coming into contact with different peoples and histories. Too often the church has confused becoming a Christian with the acceptance of practices that are allegedly universal and thus challenged "tribal" loyalties. It may be quite possible to continue to be a Sioux after being made a member of the Church of Jesus Christ. The church does not necessarily challenge such "tribalism," though it means that one can no longer kill the Pawnee because they are not Sioux. But not killing comes not from a false universal, but rather from the practice of Christian eucharist.

19. As one deeply influenced by H. Richard Niebuhr's social conception of the self, I sometimes think that those influenced by Niebuhr begin to think the very insight concerning our sociality is what the gospel is about. It is not enough to acknowledge our indebtedness to others, for what saves is not our need for community but a very particular kind of community made possible by a very particular kind of God.

20. Denny Weaver, "Atonement for the Nonconstantinian Church," *Modern Theology* 6 (July, 1990), pp. 307-23.

21. Weaver, p. 5. Weaver argues that satisfaction and substitutionary theories of the atonement tend to define the problem of the sinner in inherently individual terms. The sinner owes a debt and when the debt is paid the sinner is saved. In contrast, the *christus victor* mode of atonement is inherently social. I suspect the issues are more complex, however, as I do not think the satisfaction theories of the atonement are inescapably individualistic. The problem is the very abstraction of the idea of atonement separated from Jesus' divinity. As John Milbank suggests, "Anselm's argument is justifiable if one adds that the atonement itself, insofar as we are able to assimilate it, is only the continuation of the proclamation of the kingdom." *Theology and Social Theory: Beyond Secular Reason* (Cambridge: Basil Blackwell, 1990), p. 396.

22. John Howard Yoder, *The Priestly Kingdom: Social Ethics as Gospel* (Notre Dame: University of Notre Dame Press, 1988), p. 11. For a working out of the epistemological and ontological details of Yoder's assertion there is no better source than John Milbank's *Theology and Social Theory: Beyond Secular*

Reason. Milbank, in this book, actually does the hard work of showing how social theory that has been at the heart, particularly of Protestant theology, cannot help make the Christian ecclesial presence subordinate to the history of the West.

23. Again Milbank has made this wonderfully clear when he says, "We do not relate to the story of Christ by systematically applying its categories to the empirical content of whatever we encounter. Instead, we interpret this narrative in a response which inserts us in a narrative relation to the 'original' story. First and foremost, the Church stands in a narrative relationship to Jesus and the gospels, within a story this subsumes both. This must be the case, because no *historical* story is ever 'over and done with.' Furthermore, the New Testament itself does not preach any denial of historicity or any disappearance of our own personalities into the monistic truth of Christ. Quite to the contrary, Jesus's mission is seen as inseparable from his preaching of the kingdom and inauguration of a new sort of community, the Church. Salvation is available for us after Christ, because we can be incorporated into the community which he founded, and the response of this community to Christ is made possible by the response of the divine Spirit to the divine Son, from whom it receives the love that flows between Son and the Father. The association of the Church with a response of the Spirit which arises 'after' the Son, and yet is fully divine, shows the new community belongs from the beginning within the new narrative manifestation of God. Hence the meta-narrative is not just a story of Jesus, it is the continuing story of the Church, already realized in a finally exemplary way by Christ, yet still to be realized universally, in harmony with Christ, and yet *differently,* by all the generations of Christians." *Theology and Social Theory,* p. 387. Such claims, of course, frighten most liberal Christians because of their imperial presuppositions. The issue is not whether Christian claims are imperial, but what institutional form that takes. If you believe as I do that the church rules nonviolently, I think the questions of "imperialism" are put in quite a different context.

Moreover, Milbank is right to emphasize that salvation means reconciliation with one's fellow beings and with God. These mediations occur in the church so that the church is not primarily the means of salvation, but rather, as Milbank put it, the goal of salvation because it is the community of the reconciled. This is but to remind us that salvation as incorporation into *ecclesia* is not only social but historical. That means the individual is always saved in a particular manner according to his or her situation with regard to the Christian past and in the prospect of the Christian future. Ibid., p. 226.

24. Richard Hays, *Echoes of Scripture in the Letters of Paul* (New Haven: Yale University Press, 1989), p. 53. I think there can be no question that the Protestant emphasis upon justification by faith through grace, has resulted in a certain "gnosticizing" of the Christian gospel in Protestantism. By that I mean we were encouraged to think of the gospel primarily as a form of knowledge that could be separated from the practices of a concrete people. In such a context, theories of the atonement became too prominent as Jesus' life, cross, and resurrection was divorced from Israel. Ironically "Orthodox christologies" and liberal Protestantism

often attempt to give an account of Christianity that makes the continuation of the Jews irrelevant. Christian universalism is bought at the expense of Israel, and as a result Christians become accommodated to those stories of high humanism that ironically end up atheistic.

25. For a particularly powerful account see Nicholas Lash's "What Might Martyrdom Mean?" in his *Theology On the Way to Emmaeus* (London: SCM Press, 1986), pp. 75-94.

26. The fullest exposition of Augustine's thought by Reinhold Niebuhr is to be found in the essay, "Augustine's Political Realism," in Niebuhr's *Christian Realism and Political Problems* (New York: Charles Scribner's Sons, 1953), pp. 119-146. Niebuhr says in conclusion of the essay, "Whatever the defects of the Augustine approach may be, we must acknowledge his immense superiority both over those who precede him and who came after him. As for secular thought, it has difficulty in approaching Augustine's realism without falling into cynicism or in avoiding nihilism without falling into sentimentality. Hobbes' realism was based on an insight which he shared with Augustine, namely, that in all historical encounters the mind is the servant and not the master of the self. He failed to recognize that the self which thus made the mind its instrument was a corrupted and not a 'normal' self. Modern 'realists' know the power of collective self interest as Augustine did; but they do not understand its blindness. Modern pragmatists understood the relevance of fixed and detailed norms; but they do not understand that love must take the place as the final norm for these inadequate norms. The modern liberal Christians know that love is the final norm for man; but they fall into sentimentality because they fail to measure the power and persistence of self-love. As Augustine, whatever may be the defects of his approach to political reality and whatever may be the dangers of a too slavish devotion to his insights, nonetheless proves himself a more reliable guide than any known thinker." pp. 145-156.

   It is a fascinating hermeneutical issue how Augustine is to be interpreted. Niebuhr obviously read Augustine as a nice confirmation of his own realist views. His reading as a result was remarkably ahistorical as he read the *City of God* fundamentally as a tract in political theory. In contrast, most interpreters see the *City of God* as an extended exercise in Christian apologetics, though of course politics was intrinsic to such an apology. See, for example, Peter Kaufman, *Redeeming Politics* (Princeton: Princeton University Press, 1990), pp. 130-48.

27. Milbank notes that many commentators on Augustine, such as R. A. Markus, attempt to play down Augustine's explicit identification of the institutional church with the *City of God* and pilgrimage in the world. Yet Milbank notes that "while Augustine is certainly at pains to stress that many true members of the City of God lie outside the bonds of the institutional church, just as many of the baptized are not true members at all, this does not mean that he regards institutional inherence as a secondary and incidental matter. This is not, for example, how one should interpret Augustine's opposition to the rebaptism of returning Donatists, or his insistence, against the Donatists, of sacramental acts involving the participation of the *traditores* were not thereby contaminated or invalid. Both these oppositions in fact show that Augustine attached greater

weight than the Donatists to the public, symbolic aspects of the Catholic truth, and was critical of both their attempt to base a community entirely on a 'inward' purity of intention, and of the construal of the Catholic community in similar terms. . . . As a *civitas,* the church is, for Augustine, itself a 'political' reality. However, as the city measured more by endurance through time and by extension through space, it also has a strong 'tribal' aspect to it, which the pagan *polis* or *civitas* tended to negate. What matters is not the cultivation of excellence in the heroic present, which soon cyclically appears and disappears, but rather the ever-renewed transmission of the signs of love and the bringing to birth of new members of the womb of baptism." *Theology and Social Theory,* pp. 402-3.

28. Rowan Williams, "Politics and the Soul: A Reading of the *City of God,*" *Milltown Studies* 19/20 (1987), p. 58.

29. Ibid., p. 59.

30. Ibid., p. 61.

31. Of course as Milbank points out, Augustine simply did not have a theory of church and state. The city of this world is not a state in any modern sense of sovereignty, but rather the remains of the entire pagan mode of practice stretching back to Babylon. *Theology and Social Theory,* p. 406.

32. Williams, "Politics and the Soul: A Reading of the *City of God,*" p. 63.

33. Ibid., p. 64. As Kaufman suggests, Augustine "wanted to create 'a spiritual earthly city' somewhere between Cain's kind and the perfected City of God. He not only encouraged politicians to greater displays of piety; he also tried to shape a political culture for the spiritual earthly city that would produce the most auspicious environment for Christians to make the choices he would have them make." *The Redeeming Politics,* p. 147.

34. Williams, p. 67. Milbank, in his *Theology and Social Theory,* rightly argues that Augustine thought that for the church peace is only attained by noncoercive persuasion. However, Milbank also approves of Augustine legitimating measures of coercion outside the church. That, of course, is where I think Milbank is mistaken as well as where Augustine is mistaken. Indeed I find it hard to understand how Milbank can hold out this exception in a book that is an argument for the ontological priority of nonviolence.

2. The Politics of Justice

1. The whole issue of luck, of course, is one of the most troubling for anyone thinking seriously about a moral life. For example, John Milbank suggests in *Theology and Social Theory: Beyond Secular Reason* (Cambridge: Basil Blackwell, 1990), p. 231, "Charity also transcends the perspective of doing exact justice, of measuring up to the way things are. The supernatural perspective of charity reveals that from every finite position, within every social situation, an advance to perfection remains possible. This perspective does not simply negate the Aristotelian insight about 'moral luck,' by the way in which our moral capacities are restricted by our social situation and fortune. For the perspective is only possible as a new social perspective, which is that of the Church. To be part of the Church (insofar as it really is the Church) is to have the moral luck to belong to the society which

overcomes moral luck." I am in fundamental agreement with Milbank, but how that is to be worked out in detail is not an easy matter. For a similar set of reflections about Aristotle and luck, see my "Happiness, the Life of Virtue, and Friendship: Theological Reflections on Aristotelian Themes," *Asbury Theological Quarterly* 45, 1 (Spring 1990), pp. 5-48.

2. It is to great credit of much of the reflection being done in feminist theory today that such issues are being raised. For example, see Nancy Fraser, *Unruly Practices: Power, Discourse and Gender in Contemporary Social Theory* (Minneapolis: University of Minnesota Press, 1989). She notes concerning Richard Rorty, "There is no place in Rorty's framework for *political* motivations for the invention of new idioms, no place for idioms invented to overcome the enforced silence or muting of disadvantaged social groups. Similarly, there is no place for *collective* subjects of non-liberal discourses, hence, no place for radical discourse communities that can test dominant discourses. Finally, there is no place for *non-liberal* interpretations of social needs and collective concerns, hence, no place for, say, socialist-feminist politics. In sum, there is no place in Rorty's framework for genuinely radical political discourse rooted in oppositional solidarities" (p. 105).

3. John Rawls, *A Theory of Justice* (Cambridge: Harvard University Press, 1961), p. 63.

4. Ibid., p. 60.

5. Ibid., p. 61.

6. For Rawls's more recent reflections in defense of his theory of justice on more pragmatic grounds, see his "Justice as Fairness: Political Not Metaphysical," *Philosophy and Public Affairs* 14 (1985) and his "The Domain of Political and Overlapping Consensus," *New York University Law Review* 64, 2 (May, 1989), pp. 233-55.

7. For Rorty's defense of Rawls, see his "The Priority of Democracy to Philosophy," in the *Virginia Statute for Religious Freedom,* edited by Merrill D. Peterson and Robert C. Vaughan (Cambridge: Cambridge University Press, 1988).

8. Anthony Giddens, *The Nation-State and Violence* (Berkeley: University of California Press, 1987), p. 150.

9. Ibid., p. 172.

10. Alasdair MacIntyre, *Whose Justice? Which Rationality?* (Notre Dame: University of Notre Dame Press, 1988), pp. 1-11.

11. Ibid., p. 112.

12. Gustavo Gutiérrez, *A Theology of Liberation* (Maryknoll, New York: Orbis, 1972). My paginations are to the first edition of Gutierrez's extraordinarily important work.

13. For Gutiérrez's own account of how his work has changed since the first edition of *A Theology of Liberation,* see the introduction to the new edition (Maryknoll, New York: Orbis Books, 1988), pp. xvii-xlvi.

14. Ibid., pp. 176-77. Commenting on this passage in his introduction to the new edition of *A Theology of Liberation,* Gutiérrez says, "This idea of total liberation was inspired by that of integral development that Paul VI set down in *Populorum Progressio* (No. 21). With the help of this concept

the pope showed how it is possible, without confusing the various levels, to affirm the deep reunity of a process leading from less human to more human conditions. Among the 'more human' conditions he listed 'finally and above all: faith, a gift of God accepted by human good will, and unity and the charity of Christ, who calls us all to share his offspring in the life of the living God, the Father of all human beings.' The pope was obviously speaking of human possibilities in a broad sense, not disregarding the gratuitousness of faith and love. There is no slightest tinge of immanentism in this approach to integral liberation. But if any expression I have used may have given the impression that there is, I want to say here as forcefully as I can that any interpretation along those lines is incompatible with my position. Moreover, my repeated emphasis on the gratuitousness of God's love as the first and last word in biblical revelation is reliable evidence for this claim. The saving, all-embracing love of God is what leads me to speak of history as profoundly one (in saying this, I'm not forgetting the distinctions also to be found within history)" (pp. xxxviii-xxxix). While I deeply appreciate Gutiérrez's emphasis I do not think this necessarily solves the problems he inherited from the theological options with which he had to work. I fear that Gutiérrez's reflections on these matters has been deeply influenced by philosophical sources that, as John Milbank has characterized, "naturalize the supernatural." For Milbank's trenchant critique of some of the presuppositions behind liberation theology see his chapter 8, in *Theology and Social Theory*, pp. 206-55.

15. Gutiérrez, p. 177.

16. Ibid., p. 178.

17. Ibid., p. 146.

18. Ibid., p. 91.

19. Emmanuel Kant, *Foundations of the Metaphysics of Morals,* translated by L. W. Beck (New York: Liberal Arts Press, 1959), p. 85.

20. For further reflections on the theme of suffering, see my *Naming the Silences: God, Medicine, and the Problem of Suffering* (Grand Rapids: Wm. B. Eerdmans Publishing Co., 1990).

21. Iris Murdoch, *The Sovereignty of Good* (New York: Schocken Books, 1971), p. 80.

22. Wolfhart Pannenberg, *Christian Spirituality* (Philadelphia: Westminster Press, 1983), p. 65.

23. Ibid., p. 66.

24. Ibid., p. 70.

25. Ibid.

26. This same problem bedevils social gospel. Walter Raschenbusch, to his credit, was quite clear that his views were clearly theocratic that he assumed that theocracy was perfectly institutionalized in democracy. That, of course, is exactly the question at issue. See his *Righteousness of the Kingdom*, edited by Max Stackhouse (Nashville: Abingdon Press, 1968), pp. 79-98.

27. Pannenberg, *Christian Spirituality* pp. 89-91.

28. John Langan, S.J., "What Jerusalem Says to Athens," *The Faith That Does Justice,* edited by John Haughey (New York: Paulist Press, 1977), pp. 152-53.

29. See, for example, Harlan Beckley, "A Christian Affirmation of Rawls' Idea of Justice as Fairness: Part I," *The Journal of Religious Ethics* 13, 2 (Fall 1986), pp. 210-42; and Part II in *The Journal of Religious Ethics* 14, 2 (Fall 1988), pp. 229-46. See also the response by Greg Jones, "Should Christians Affirm Rawls' Justice as Fairness?," *The Journal of Religious Ethics* 16, 2 (Fall 1988), pp. 251-71.

30. R. H. Tawney, *Equality* (London: Allen & Unwin, 1979), p. 167.

31. Michael Sandel, *Liberalism and the Limits of Justice* (Cambridge: University of Cambridge Press, 1982), p. 172.

32. Michael Ignatieff, *The Needs of Strangers* (New York: Viking, 1985). See also Nancy Fraser's extraordinary chapter in *Unruly Practices: Struggle Over Needs*, pp. 161-87. In "The Origins of Duty," *Harper's Magazine* (February, 1991), Christopher Lasch observes, "Much of what was considered a citizen's duty [in America] was built upon the Jeffersonian assumption of a broad distribution of property ownership, especially agrarian property. The management of property was believed to confer the habits of initiative, enterprise, and responsibility, which were essential to citizenship. But industrialism gave rise to a class of permanent, propertyless wage earners, estranged by their condition from the wellspring of civic virtue: proprietorship. How Jeffersonian virtue can be reconciled with this unforeseen development remains a problem no one has resolved. The culture of consumption has made this problem even more complicated. The rise of consumerism in this century—in which the individual's self-interest is the *only* good—created a society in which you don't need any public consensus as long as the economy can satisfy people's needs and expand them into ever increasing levels of desire and expectation. Beguiled by the prospects of limitless abundance, Americans came to believe that it was no longer necessary to grapple with underlying issues of justice and equality as long as the goods kept coming" (p. 45).

33. Robert Nozick, *Anarchy, State and Utopia* (New York: Basic Books, 1974).

34. Alasdair MacIntyre, *After Virtue* (Notre Dame: University of Notre Dame Press, 1984), pp. 250-51.

35. Lesslie Newbigin, *Foolishness to Greeks: The Gospel in Western Culture* (Grand Rapids: Eerdmans, 1986), p. 76.

36. Ibid., p. 19.

37. Ibid., p. 33.

38. MacIntyre, *After Virtue*, p. 106.

39. Giddens, *The Nation-State and Violence*, pp. 180-81. For a critique of modern social science similar to Giddens', see Milbank, *Theology and Social Theory*, pp. 75-100. Milbank makes clear that sociology has become justification of the very societies that have produced the necessity of something called sociology.

40. Newbigin, *Foolishness to Greeks* p. 27.

41. Giddens, *The Nation State and Violence* p. 210.

42. Ibid., p. 234.

43. Ibid., p. 113.

44. Ibid., p. 114.

45. Ibid., p. 250.
46. After this essay was finished, Duncan B. Forrester's "Political Justice and Christian Theology" appeared in *Studies in Christian Ethics: Political Ethics* 3, 1 (Edinburgh: T & T Clark, 1990), pp. 1-13. Forrester there argues a case much like the one I develop here.

3. The Politics of Freedom

1. For two classic studies of the question of church and state in America see John Bennett, *Christians and the State* (New York: Charles Scribners and Sons, 1958) and John Courtney Murray, *We Hold These Truths* (Garden City, New York: Image Books, 1964). Both these books are excellent, yet both deal primarily with the question of how to interpret the status of freedom of religion in America rather than how the church can remain free in America. Questions of how to interpret the First Amendment are obviously important both legally and socially. Yet, if we let our attention be directed entirely to that issue, we can fail to see that the church has already subordinated itself to state interests.

2. For an excellent analysis of Jefferson's, Madison's, and Williams's views on the First Amendment, see William Lee Miller, *The First Liberty: Religion and the American Republic* (New York: Alfred Knopf, 1986). Miller nicely demonstrates that the "snappy formula" that "Jefferson believed in separation to protect the state from the church, but Roger Williams believed in it to protect the church from the state," is memorable but suffers from the small problem of being mistaken. Williams simply did not understand that the church that is "separate" from the state is an actual, visible church, since—as Miller points out—Williams was as suspicious of the power of visible churches as he was the power of the state (pp. 182-83). Of course on that issue hangs much of our later history, as the very individualism encouraged by such ecclesiologies is the acid through which the church is left powerless to qualify the power of the state.

    I call attention to Ellul's book because, like most of his work, it is maddeningly suggestive. For he suggests the subversion of Christianity is best seen in the creation of the very idea of Christianity which becomes a "philosophy" that one can accept without dealing with Jesus. Once the transition is made from history to philosophy, Christians forget the essential point "that God does not reveal by means of a philosophical system or a moral code or a metaphysical construction. He enters human history and accompanies his people. The Hebrew Bible is not a philosophical construction or a system of knowledge. It is a series of stories that are not myths intended to veil or unveil objective and abstract truths. These stories are *one history*, the history of the people of God." *The Subversion of Christianity*, trans. by Geoffrey Bromiley (Grand Rapids: William Eerdmans, 1986), p. 23. What is useful about Ellul's point is that there does seem to be a connection between the failure to take the historic particularity of God's action in Israel and Jesus seriously and Christianity becoming a civil religion. I suspect that the conceptual and historical linkages to explain this relation are more complex than Ellul's book indicates.

3. Christopher Mooney, *Public Virtue: Law and the Social Character of Religion* (Notre Dame: University of Notre Dame, 1986), p. 27. Mooney continues

with the observation that "the churches have become confused in regard to what should be their primary religious witness in a pluralistic land. For institutional religion usually suffers from one of two types of irrelevance: either it retains meaning for its members on the personal level but loses it for society at large, or it manages to be historically relevant in the public realm but of little or no significance for the needs of ordinary people. This is because the American value system has always been a mixture of the secular and the sacred, and American religion has generally exhibited the same sort of value mix. Churches and synagogues were able to cope so easily with the secularization of the twentieth century precisely because to a certain extent they had incorporated many of society's secular values into their own systems of thought and bureaucratic structures" (pp. 17-28). Mooney provides an excellent discussion of recent decisions involving the First Amendment.

4. Miller, p. vii.

5. John Wilson, "Common Religion in American Society," in *Civil Religion and Political Theology* (Notre Dame: University of Notre Dame Press, 1986), pp.112-13.

6. Miller, p. 350. Miller's discussion of the crucial court cases involving questions of freedom of religion and their relation to the larger questions is extremely illuminating exactly because Miller himself seems unsure how to resolve the dilemma of providing for freedom of religion without establishing some religion as dominant. The history of Supreme Court decisions on these matters is a good illustration of the American tendency to deal with what are essentially political questions through the legal system. As a result, we constantly ask more of the legal enterprise than it is capable of giving.

7. Miller, p. 233.

8. I wrote this essay when Rorty's paper was still in manuscript. My pagination references in the text are to that version. The paper has subsequently been published in *The Virginia Statute for Religious Freedom*, ed. by Merrill Peterson and Robert C. Vaughn (Cambridge: Cambridge University Press, 1988).

9. Rorty's reference is to John Rawls, "Justice as Fairness: Political Not Metaphysical," *Philosophy and Public Affairs* 14 (1985).

10. Rorty helpfully points out that Rawls in *A Theory of Justice* comments on Loyola's attempt to make the love of God the "dominant good." "Although to subordinate all our aims to one end does not strictly speaking violate the principles of rational choice. . . . it still strikes us as irrational, or more likely as mad" (553-54). This is, of course, consistent with Rawls's earlier claim that "a well-ordered society tends to eliminate or at least to control men's inclinations to injustice" so that "warring and intolerant sects are much less likely to exist" (247). It is interesting to note how fearful people like Rorty and Rawls can be of conflict.

11. William Bennett, "Religious Belief and the Constitutional Order," in *Religious Beliefs, Human Rights, and the Moral Foundation of Western Democracy*, ed. by Carl H. Esbeck (Columbia: University of Missouri, 1986). Paginations in the text.

12. Though it will be obvious from the below that I have little sympathy with Bennett's case, I must admit I find shocking the way American history is now taught in our public schools so that no one's religious sensibilities are disturbed. This will be the focus of the last chapter.

13. I assume that Bennett thinks that those who are ready to die for their country are also those who are ready to kill. It seems never to occur to him that there might be some tension between the virtues intrinsic to the Christian faith and those he thinks necessary for the preservation of America.

   I cannot resist calling attention to another speech quoted by Arthur Cochrane, *The Mystery of Peace* (Elgin, Illinois: Brethren Press, 1986), p. 135. It is not too unlike that of former Secretary Bennett, though it was given earlier in this century and in a different country. This political leader on assuming office said, "The national Government sees in the two Christian Confessions the most important factors for the preservation of our nationality. It will respect the agreements that have been drawn up between them and the provincial states. Their rights are not to be infringed. It expects, however, and hopes that conversely, the work upon the national and moral renewal of our nation, which the Government has assumed as its task, will receive the same appreciation. The national Government will provide and guarantee to the Christian Confessions the influence due them in the schools and education. It is concerned for genuine harmony between Church and State. The struggle against materialism and for the establishment of a true community in the nation serves just as much as the interests of the nation as it does those of our Christian faith." So spoke Adolf Hitler, March 23, 1933. I cheated a bit—in the original quotation the last sentence reads, "The Struggle against materialism and for the establishment of a true community in the *German* nation serves just as much the interests of the nation as it does those of our Christian faith." I certainly would not suggest that former Secretary Bennett is rightly associated with Hitler, but rather only note how quickly virtue can serve destructive forces.

14. Bennett's appeal to the "Judeo-Christian" morality is almost comical if it were not so serious. That hyphen is the result of Enlightenment accounts of religion that assume that the more "universal" Christian religion subsumed the best in Judaism. From such a perspective the fact that Judaism still exists is intelligible only as necessary background for understanding Christianity.

15. John Waide, "Freedom of Religion: A Failure of American Philosophy" (unpublished paper).

16. This is quite a different issue from whether Jews (and most Christians) want their children freely to believe. The "Called Churches'" commitment to noncoercive belief is not the same as "making it possible for people to choose to believe or not."

17. On this point see the remarkable essay by Jean Bethke Elshtain, "Citizenship and Armed Civic Virtue: Some Critical Questions on the Commitment to Public Life," *Soundings* 69, nos. 1-2 (Spring/Summer 1986), pp. 99-110.

18. Robert Bellah, "Public Philosophy and Public Theology in America Today," in *Civil Religion and Political Theology*, pp. 79-97 and Richard John

Neuhaus, "From Civil Religion to Public Philosophy," in *Civil Religion and Political Theology*, pp. 98-110. Bellah expresses agreement with Neuhaus's position as developed in *The Naked Public Square* but has reservations about Neuhaus's proposition, "On balance and considering the alternative, the influence of the United States is a force for good in the world." He suggests that such a proposition limits the kind of critical patriotism he thinks necessary. Yet I find such a disavowal of Neuhaus's proposition puzzling given Bellah's own commitments about America with which he should be in agreement.

For Neuhaus's criticism of Rorty, see his "Joshing Richard Rorty," *First Things* 8 (December, 1990), pp. 14-24.

19. Neuhaus, p. 103. Both Bellah's and Neuhaus's call for a critical patriotism is insufficiently developed as I suspect what they have in mind is not patriotism at all. As Alasdair MacIntyre has argued in his "Is Patriotism a Virtue?," it is not patriotism to argue that one's nation's cause is one to which we should be loyal because it is a grand moral ideal, for then it is the ideal and not the nation that is the object of regard, and thus there is no reason why someone who is not a member of the nation should uphold that nation's cause. In contrast, MacIntyre argues that patriotism is "defined in terms of a kind of loyalty to a particular nation which only those possessing that particular nationality can exhibit." "The Lindley Lecture" (University of Kansas, March 26, 1984. Published by Department of Philosophy), pp. 3-4.

20. For still another good attempt to provide a positive account of the relation of religion to our social order, see Robin Lovin, "Religion and American Public Life: Three Relationships," in *Religion and American Public Life*, ed. by Robin Lovin (New York: Paulist Press, 1986), pp. 7-28. Lovin makes the interesting suggestion that a serious concern for religion and social justice must begin by confronting the problem of pluralism. For some basis must be found to show how a system of ideas centered on a distinctive set of theological affirmations can be understood and even criticized by an observer who stands initially within another system. If religion took this public role it would strengthen the society "which mediates between the particular communities of identity and the general coercive power of the state. In an American culture which seems to be more threatened internally by a positivism which drains public life of meaning than by a totalitarianism which loads it with an imposed and exclusive system of meanings, religion's most important public role may be to strengthen the society by a vigorous use of that forum, stressing the importance of questions that can be resolved neither by the power of the state nor in the confines of particular communities" (pp. 25-26). I am a good deal less hopeful than Lovin, but I have no in-principled reason to object to Lovin's project though I think his claim that "recent theological reflection on language provides an explanation of the conditions that make such public truth possible" is exaggerated—consider Rorty above.

21. James Gustafson's chapter "The Voluntary Church: A Moral Appraisal" in his *The Church as Moral Decision Maker* (Philadelphia: Pilgrim Press, 1970), pp. 109-38 is an astute analysis of this problem.

22. Max Stackhouse, "Piety, Polity, and Policy," in *Religious Beliefs, Human Rights, and the Moral Foundation of Western Democracy*, p. 23.

23. Ibid., p. 25. This understanding of theology sounds very much like Enlightenment ideology.

24. Ibid., p. 13.

25. Of course on this large claim, as they say, hangs the tale—a tale I cannot develop here. At best all I can do is call your attention to the statement by G. B. Caird about Jesus' death, "He goes to his death at the hands of a Roman judge on a charge of which he was innocent and his accusers, as the event proved, were guilty. And so, not only in theological truth but in historic fact, the one bore the sins of the many confident that in him the whole Jewish nation was being nailed to the cross, only to come to life again in a better resurrection, and that the Day of the Son of Man which would see the end of the old Israel would see also the vindication of the new." This is quoted by N. T. Wright in his article, "Jesus, Israel, and the Cross," *SBL 1985 Seminar Papers* (Atlanta: Scholars Press, 1985), p. 93. It is my suspicion that more "sacrificial" atonement theories in which Jesus' "Jewishness" is forgotten correlates with the necessity to turn Christianity into a civil religion.

26. I do not deny that "the people" may in fact rule in America, though I am unsure if we even know what that means or should mean, but rather I am challenging the assumption that a more truthful society is one in which the people rule. For extended reflection on my understanding of the challenges facing the church in our society, see my *Christian Existence Today: Essays on Church, World and Living in Between* (Durham, North Carolina: Labyrinth Press, 1988) and in particular chapter 9, "A Christian Critique of Christian America."

27. It has not been the burden of this essay to try to suggest an alternative institutional arrangement for this society to deal with the problem of the diverse religious groups. As a start I would favor calling the state policy we have "religious tolerance" or "state religious tolerance," thus making clear that the state is not granting "religious freedom."

4. The Politics of Church

1. *The Circuit Rider* 24 (March, 1989). The letter was signed by Dennis Groh of Evanston, Illinois.

2. I think Lindbeck's account of the experiential expressivist model in his *The Nature of Doctrine: Religion and Theology in a Post Liberal Age* (Philadelphia: Westminster Press, 1984) fails to give an adequate account of the material factors that make the experiential expressivist model so powerful. Experiential expressivism is almost required by the privatization of people's lives that goes hand in hand with political liberalism and capitalist economy. Even more conservative denominations, therefore, in spite of what they may hold explicitly, end up in some form of experiential expressivism.

3. The phrase *life-style enclave* I obviously have borrowed from Robert Bellah and his coauthors in their *Habits of the Heart: Individualism and Commitment in American Life* (Berkeley: University of California Press, 1985).

4. Robert Wuthnow, *The Restructuring of American Religion: Society and Faith Since World War II* (Princeton: Princeton University Press, 1988).

5. The originator of this peculiar blend of Christian social action with individualistic accounts of Christian salvation was, of course, Reinhold Niebuhr. In an odd way Niebuhr moved away from the social gospel exactly at the wrong point, as he gave what was an essentially Lutheran understanding of salvation in opposition to the more Calvinistic strains of the social gospel. Niebuhr, in effect, was the Lutheran law gospel distinction in American pragmatic dress.

6. MacIntyre notes that the assumption of the eighteenth-century moralists was that there was a universality of moral agreement about fundamentals in ethics. They were not unaware, however, that often there were differences between cultures, but these differences were thought to derive from different application of the same set of moral rules in different circumstances. This was combined with a belief in progress, so that some societies were obviously further along than others concerning more appropriate application of the basic rules which all shared. The purpose of moral theory in such a world is not just recording and protecting the judgments of the plain person, but the constructive text "of organizing and harmonizing the moral beliefs of plain persons in the manner best calculated to secure a rational sense from the largest possible number of such persons, independently of their conflicting views upon other matters. The moral philosopher's aim, then, is, or ought to be, that of articulating a rational consensus out of the pre-theoretical beliefs and judgments of plain persons." *Three Rival Versions of Moral Inquiry: Encyclopedia, Genealogy and Tradition* (Notre Dame: University of Notre Dame Press, 1990), pp. 176-77. Modern moral philosophy from this perspective is a necessary correlative to the attempt to develop democratic societies that organize people irrespective of their moral training. I suspect that is the reason why some are beginning to see more commonality between Aristotelianism and Christianity because in spite of their deep differences, they are both equally antidemocratic.

7. For a further development of this, see my "Honor in the University," *First Things* 10 (February, 1991), pp. 26-31.

8. I am aware that such a claim appears authoritarian, but ironically I think it is just the opposite of authoritarianism. What does it mean to introduce students to think like me? It means I must introduce them to all the sources that think through me, and in the process they will obviously learn to think not only like me, but different from me as the different voices that think through me provide them with skills I have not appropriated sufficiently.

9. Klinkers were those bricks that were at the bottom of the kilns and they were therefore often overfired. They would sometimes have interesting projections that made quite beautiful walls. The difficulty with klinkers is they were extremely hard and therefore when you laid them, they could float on the mortar. Often bricklayers without much experience would find it very hard to lay klinkers because they were almost impossible to lay level over an entire course. The relationship between the consistency of the brick and the consistency of the mortar is a matter to which bricklayers constantly have to adjust. For example, how you lay brick at the midpoint of the day may be a bit different from how you lay brick early in the morning, as the

sun is not out in full force and the mortar does not dry out as quickly. So in the morning you might be able to spread your mud further along the course than you can at midday.

10. George Will's *Men at Work: The Craft of Baseball* (New York: Macmillan Publishing Co., 1990) strikes me as a wonderful book in moral philosophy. The book really is about craft and how discipline is required to make the craft one's own. I must admit as I read through the book I thought I might catch Will distorting baseball by his own liberal presuppositions. The first chapters are primarily about individuals such as managers, pitchers, and hitters. However, Will clearly denotes the communitarian aspects of baseball in his chapter on the defense. It is a book well worth contemplating.

11. MacIntyre suggests "Moral inquiry moves toward arriving at theoretical and practical conclusions about [particular] virtues. But one cannot learn how to move toward such a conclusion without first having acquired some at least of those same virtues about which one is inquiring and without therefore having first been able to identify which virtues they are and, to at least some minimal extent, what it is about them which makes these particular habits virtues. So we are threatened by an apparent paradox and an understanding of moral inquiry as a type of craft: only insofar as we have already arrived at certain conclusion are we able to become the sort of person able to engage in such inquiry so as to reach sound conclusions. How was this threat a paradox—recognizably a version of that posed at the outset by Plato and the *Meno* about learning in general—to be circumvented, dissolved, or otherwise met? The answer is in part that suggested by the *Meno:* unless we already have within ourselves potentiality for moving toward and achieving the relevant theoretical and practical conclusions, we shall be unable to learn. But we also need a teacher to enable us to actualize that potentiality, and we shall have to learn from that teacher and initially accept on the basis of his or her authority within the community of a craft precisely what intellectual and moral habits it is which we must cultivate and acquire if we are to become effective self-moved participants in such inquiries. Hence there emerges a conception of rational teaching authority internal to the practice of the craft of moral inquiry, as indeed such a conception emerge in such other crafts as furniture making and fishing, where, just as in moral inquiry, they partially define relationships with master-craftsmen to apprentice." *Three Rival Versions of Moral Inquiry,* p. 63.

12. For my reflections on this circular account, see my "Happiness, the Life of Virtue, and Friendship: Theological Reflections on Aristotelian Themes," *Asbury Theological Journal* 45, no. 1 (Spring 1990), pp. 21-35.

13. MacIntyre, *Three Rival Versions of Moral Inquiry,* pp. 61-62.

14. MacIntyre's epistemological views are more determinatively developed in the latter chapters of *Whose Justice? Which Rationality?* (Notre Dame: University of Notre Dame Press, 1988). There MacIntyre says, "The original and most elementary version of the correspondence theory of truth is one in which it is applied retrospectively in the form of a correspondence theory of falsity. The first question to be raised about it is: what is it precisely that corresponds or fails to correspond to what?

Assertions in speech are written, certainly, but these as secondary expressions of intelligent thought which is or is not adequate in its dealings with its objects, the realities of the social and rational world. This is a point at which it is important to remember that the presupposed conception of mind is not Cartesian. It is rather of mind as activity, of mind as engaging with the natural and social world in such activities as identification, reidentification, collecting, separating, classifying, and naming in all this by touching, grasping, pointing, breaking down, building up, calling to, answering to, and so on. The mind is adequate with objects insofar as the expectation which it frames on the basis of these activities are not liable to disappointment and remembering which it engages in enables it to return and recover what it had encountered previously, whether the objects themselves are still present or not. The mind, being informed as a result of its engagements with the objects, is informed by both images which are or are not adequate—for the mind's purposes, re-presentations of particular objects or sorts of objects and by contrast which are or are not adequate re-presentations of the form in terms of which objects are grasped and classified. Representation is not as such picturing, but re-presentation. Pictures are only one mode of re-presenting, and their adequacy or inadequacy in functioning as such is always relative to some specific purposes in mind. One of the great originating insights of tradition—constituted inquiries is that false beliefs and false judgments represent the failure of mind, not of its objects. This falsity is recognized retrospectively as a past inadequacy when the discrepancy between the beliefs of an earlier stage of tradition of inquiry are contrasted with the world of things and persons as it has come to be understood at some later stage. So correspondence or lack of it becomes a feature of developing complex conceptions of truth. The relationship of correspondence or lack of correspondence which holds between the mind and objects is given expression in judgments, but it is not judgments themselves which correspond to the objects or indeed to anything else" (pp. 356-57). Of course, the strength of MacIntyre's position is to deny the epistemological starting point of the Enlightenment tradition. That is why he must so starkly juxtapose traditions as the Augustinian-Thomistic tradition does not assume it must secure a starting point epistemologically in order to begin reflection. Thus the very structure of the *summa* as a disputation rightly indicates there is no place to start. This has deep implications for the style of philosophical and theological work since it becomes crucial that we find a form that unsettles the Enlightenment presumption that truth can be presented in a lecture and/or essay. Thus I must learn to write theology in a way that denies that theology can be systematic.

15. MacIntyre, *Three Rival Versions of Moral Inquiry,* pp. 64-65.

16. Ibid., p. 128. MacIntyre argues that philosophy necessarily must become the master craft if our hierarchies are to be rational. There I fear he and I may well be in disagreement, depending on what he means by philosophy since I necessarily must argue that theology, not philosophy, is in service to a community that ultimately must claim philosophy as a servant.

17. Again Reinhold Niebuhr is the great representative of this tendency in modern theology. There is no question, moreover, it was a powerful apologetic strategy as long as one could presume the lingering habits of a Christian civilization. However, those habits now seem to me to be gone for good and with good riddance. This issue again is nicely illustrated by Martha Nussbaum's review of MacIntyre's *Whose Justice? Which Rationality?* titled "Recoiling from Reason," *New York Review of Books* 36, no. 19 (December 7, 1989), pp. 36-41. In that review she accuses MacIntyre of introducing the concept of sin to underwrite an authoritarian politics, and in this case a church, that cannot but offend any rational account of human existence. In contrast, Nussbaum argues that we must recover Aristotle without Christian eyes because only then are we capable of securing the kind of rational agreement necessary to sustain modern liberal society. Thus she says, "This is not to minimize the difficulty of going beyond recognition of common experience in problems to construct common norms. With each step such an inquiry should balance the concrete experience of particular groups with an interest in what is common to all. How one might do this remains an immensely challenging question, but I see no reason to suppose that it cannot be done. If the doctrine of original sin, as MacIntyre interprets it, were true, the obstacles in the way of carrying out such a project would be formidable, since presumably original sin impedes the reasoning of each reasoner, as well as making it difficult for a reasoned view to win acceptance. But MacIntyre has given us no good reason to believe that doctrine is true. And unless and until we accept some such idea we do not have reason to relax our demands for good reasons, deferring to authority" (p. 41). Though I think Nussbaum is wrong to assume that an account of sin is meant to underwrite an authoritarian politics, she is surely right to argue that those committed to the grand liberal project should reject any notion of sin. For a more extended discussion of Nussbaum see my "Can Aristotle Be a Liberal? Nussbaum on Luck," *Soundings* 72, no. 4 (Winter 1989), pp. 675-92.

18. One of the great problems after Protestantism lost the confessional was any ability to know how to name sins as sins. It is one of the great riches of the Catholic tradition that it is able to locate avarice, greed, lust, theft, adultery, and murder in a tradition that gives them a rational display as sin. As Protestants we have lost the ability to name our sins and thus lack the kind of discerning practices to have our lives located within the narrative of the church. For further reflections in this respect see my "Casuistry in Context," *Experience in Medicine,* ed. by Warren Reich (forthcoming).

5. The Politics of Sex

1. *Human Sexuality: New Directions in American Catholic Thought,* A study commissioned by the Catholic Theological Society of America. Anthony Kosnik, chairperson (New York: Paulist Press, 1977). All pagination references to this report will appear in the text.

2. Catherine MacKinnon, "Feminism, Marxism, Method, and the State: An Agenda for Theory," *The Signs Reader,* ed. by Elizabeth Abel and Emile Abel (Chicago: University of Chicago Press, 1983), p. 243. For MacKinnon's fuller views, see her *Toward a Feminist Theory of the State* (Cambridge: Harvard University Press, 1989).

3. MacKinnon, "Feminism, Marxism, Method, and the State: An Agenda for Theory," p. 244.

4. Bertrand Russell, *Marriage and Morals* (New York: Liverwright, 1957). All pagination references will be in the text.

5. Robert Nisbet, *The Quest for Community* (London: Oxford University Press, 1953), pp. 60-61.

6. *The Church Speaks to the Modern World: The Social Teachings of Leo XIII*, ed. by Etienne Gilson (New York: Image Books, 1954), p. 97. That Leo could make such a claim about marriage, of course, was because he assumed that the church knew better than the state what marriage is.

7. Bertrand Russell, *Marriage and Morals*, p. 176.

8. For more extensive reflections on these matters see my *A Community of Character: Toward a Constructive Christian Social Ethics* (Notre Dame: University of Notre Dame Press, 1981), pp. 155-95. Janet Fishburn's *Confronting the Idolatry of Family: A New Vision for the Household of God* (Nashville: Abingdon Press, 1991) is a welcome alternative to the forging of family by more Christians.

9. One of the ironies of neoconservative defenses of the family is their correlative support of capitalism. They assume that capitalism creates a private space that is not subject to the market. Therefore they make much of distinctions between the economic realm, the political realm, and the cultural realm. They assume the family is part of the cultural realm and therefore not to be understood in the same terms as our economic relationships. That, of course, fails to recognize capitalism's inherent drive to make all relationships contractual. Just as capitalism wants to de-territorialize all human relations, so it must also try to undermine all particularistic commitments that are not a manifestation of freedom as determined by the market. So ironically neoconservatives work to create an economic order that can only undermine those institutions that they allegedly care the most about. On the necessity of de-territorialization as the essence of capitalism, see John Milbank, *Theology and Social Theory: Beyond Secular Reason* (Cambridge: Basil Blackwell, 1990), pp. 273-74.

10. For a fuller account of this understanding of what it means to be a creature, see my *The Peaceable Kingdom: A Primer in Christian Ethics* (Notre Dame: University of Notre Dame Press, 1983).

11. For more extended reflections on the nature and importance of friendship for Christians see my "Happiness, the Life of Virtue, and Friendship: Theological Reflections on Aristotelian Themes," *The Asbury Theological Journal* 45, no. 1 (Spring 1990), pp. 35-44.

6. The Politics of Witness

1. Indeed, as MacIntyre makes clear, in both *Whose Justice? Which Rationality?* (Notre Dame: University of Notre Dame Press, 1988) and *Three Rival Versions of Moral Inquiry: Encyclopedia, Genealogy and Tradition* (Notre Dame: University of Notre Dame Press, 1990), perhaps the most determinative characteristic of modernity is its presumption that there is no "otherness" that is not capable of being understood if we just work hard enough at it. I

suspect this accounts for the stress on otherness associated with such extraordinary thinkers as Adorno, but one of the difficulties with the abstract category of otherness is how it tends to domesticate that which we fear. However, there can be no question of the significance of the category of the other as a challenge to the presumptions of Enlightenment rationality.

For an attack on the language of pluralism, which so often embodies the assumption of our ability to "understand the other," see John Milbank, "The End of Dialogue," in *Christian Uniqueness Reconsidered: The Myth of a Pluralistic Theology of Religion*, ed. by Gavin D'Costa (Maryknoll, New York: Orbis Books, 1990), pp. 174-91. Milbank contends that the "terms of discourse which provide both the favored categories for encounter with other religions—dialogue, pluralism, and the like—together with the criteria for the acceptable limits of the pluralist embrace—social justice, liberation, and so forth—are themselves embedded in a wider Western discourse become globally dominant. And the implication of this paradox is evident: The moment of contemporary recognition of other cultures and religions optimistically celebrated by this volume, is itself—as the rhetoric of its celebration makes apparent—none other than the moment of total obliteration of other cultures by Western norms and categories, with their freight of Christian influence. That yoking the good causes of socialism, feminism, anti-racism, and ecologism to the concerns of pluralism, actually tends to curb and confine them, because the discourse of pluralism exerts a rhetorical drag in a so-called liberal direction, which assumes the propriety of the West-inspired nation-state and the West-inspired capitalist economy" (p. 175). As Milbank asks later, "How can a consensus about social justice, which is relatively independent of religion, possibly help to mediate the differences between religions?" (p. 182). For an equally compelling challenge see Ken Surin, "A 'Politics of Speech:' Religious Pluralism in the Age of the McDonald's Hamburger," in D'Costa, pp. 192-212.

2. MacIntyre, *Whose Justice? Which Rationality?*, p. 373.

3. Ibid., p. 378.

4. Stephen Fowl argues that MacIntyre has overstated his case concerning translation by confusing translatability with acceptability. He follows Stout's arguments, drawing on Donald Davidson, to argue "that for any group of expressionists to which we ascribe the term *language*, there must be sufficient overlap with our own expressions to allow analogies to be drawn and translations to begin. If there were absolutely no parallels between another group's expressions and our own, we would lack sufficient reason for ascribing the term *language* to their expressions." "Could Horace Talk With the Hebrews? Translatability and Moral Disagreement in MacIntyre and Stout," *Journal of Religion Ethic* 19, no. 1 (Fall 1991). The quote comes from pages 5-6 of the manuscript copy. Fowl's point is not, however, to undermine MacIntyre's general position in favor of Stout's in *Ethics After Babel* (Boston: Beacon Press, 1988), but rather to indicate that total disagreement on any issue is impossible. I am not as convinced, however, as Fowl (and Stout) are by Davidson's general arguments concerning incommensurability. As Michael Quirk points out, Davidson tends to think of language fundamentally as a locus of belief. He thus fails to note that languages depend on what Wittgenstein calls "agreements and judgments."

That is only made possible against a background of skills and practices. That, I take it, is the heart of MacIntyre's position on these matters. Quirk's views are in his paper, "Stout on Relativism, Liberalism, and Communitarianism," *Auslegung* 17, no. 1 (Winter 1991), pp. 1-14.

Milbank agrees with Fowl that it is certainly the case that there must be some background of agreements for a radical disagreement to even be possible, yet that in no way undermines MacIntyre's primary point that denies "an outsider's knowledge is just equivalent to that of an insider; the difference is small, but vital. For the outsider can know all the rules, even the rules for modifying the rules, in many circumstances will be able to predict the behavior of the cultural aliens. However, he will be unlikely to have the ability for 'poetic' innovation, or to be able to predict this, precisely because a sense of continuity—indifference involves an inprescribable judgment which necessitates belief in the condition in question 'is going somewhere,' pressing towards a *telos* that it can never adequately express in words. The outsider, being by definition a nonbeliever in this imminent/transcendent directionality, will only be able to make innovations which he finds 'attractive' in a playful spirit, but is bound to see these as essentially arbitrary departures, not further specifications of an elusive *telos*. . . . So, for an alien tongue to be comprehensible to us need not mean that we have found some linguistic equivalent, merely that we have begun to be ourselves alien to our former selves through the process encountered." John Milbank, *Theology and Social Theory: Beyond Secular Reason* (Cambridge: Basil Blackwell, 1990), pp. 341-42.

5. MacIntyre, *Whose Justice? Which Rationality?*, p. 382. By introducing the poetic, MacIntyre does not mean that innovation in a language can only be accomplished by poets since knowing how to go on and to go further in the language is potentially an ability that every language user is capable. The poet thus names some who have that ability in a peculiar degree.

6. Ibid., p. 373.

7. Michael J. Shapiro, *The Politics of Representation* (Madison: University of Wisconsin Press, 1988), p. 107. He is quoting Tyvetan Todorov, *The Conquest of America*, trans. by Richard Howard (New York: Harper Torchbooks, 1987), p. 5.

8. Shapiro, p. 108.

9. Ibid., pp. 109-10. Glen Olsen objects that Shapiro's description of the Spanish as "socially self-centered" fails to do justice to the Spanish consciencious to provide justification, which often required sacrifice of their own interests, for their mission.

10. Ibid., p. 109.

11. Todorov, *The Conquest of America*, pp. 168-69.

12. Shapiro, p. 95. It may be objected that Shapiro's evidence in this respect is weighted since people in Utah generally live longer than most Americans. The reason is that they are Mormons who do not engage in practices for religious reasons that are so disastrous for health of the general population. Yet Shapiro's point remains valid because it is hard to see how anyone could fail to acknowledge that Native Americans are in a decided

disadvantage in this country to the extent that they determine to remain Native Americans.

13. Michel de Certeau notes how maps, particularly in the Middle Ages, are structured on the travel story: "stories of journeys and actions are marked out by the 'citation' of the places that result from them or authorize them. From this angle, we can compare the combination of 'tours' and 'maps' in everyday stories with the manner in which, over the past five centuries, they have been interlaced and then slowly disassociated in literary and scientific representations of space. In particular, if one takes the 'map' in its current geographical form, we can see that in the course of the period marked by the birth of modern scientific discourse (i.e., from the 15th-17th century) the map has slowly disengaged itself from the itineraries that were the conditions of its possibility." *The Practice of Everyday Life* (Berkeley: University of California Press, 1984), p. 120. De Certeau's reflections on the relationship between stories and space, as well as time and place, provide a fascinating way to rethink the strong distinctions between history and nature so prevalent in our modern discourse.

I am indebted to Phil Kenneson for calling my attention to this extraordinary book.

14. Lesslie Newbigin, *Foolishness to the Greeks: The Gospel in Western Culture* (Grand Rapids: Eerdmans, 1986), p. 140.

15. Ibid., p. 140.

16. MacIntyre notes, "The commonest candidate, in modern versions of what is all too often taken to be *the* correspondent theory of truth, for that which corresponds to a judgment in this way is a fact. But facts, like telescopes and wigs for gentlemen, were a 17th-century invention. In the 16th century and earlier 'fact' in English was usually a rendering of the Latin 'factum,' a deed, in action, and sometimes in Scholastic Latin an event on occasion. It was only in the 17th-century that 'fact' was first used in a way in which later philosophers such as Russell, Wittgenstein, and Ramsey were to use it. It is of course and always was harmless, philosophically and otherwise to use the word 'fact' of what a judgment states. What is and was not harmless, but highly misleading, was to conceive of a realm of facts independent of judgment or any other form of linguistic expression, so that judgments or statements or sentences could be paired off with facts, truth or falsity being alleged relationship between such paired items." *Whose Justice? Which Rationality?* pp. 357-58. To continue to use, therefore, value language only underwrites this sense of the factual which seems so clearly wrong.

17. Newbigin, *Foolishness to the Greeks: The Gospel in Western Culture*, p. 38.

18. These are obviously more complex questions than can be treated adequately here. It is my own view, however, that part of the difficulty is our acceptance of the term *nature* as having more descriptive power than the Christian affirmation of creation. Things go decisively wrong when nature is understood primarily as a contrast to human rather than to God. Creation rightly reminds us that all being has a created status that is in service.

19. This advertisement appeared on page 17 of *The New York Review of Books.* I

have subsequently learned that this is the National Association of Scholars' statement of purpose. It has been widely distributed across universities.

20. The first drafts of this chapter were written in May of 1990. When I selected the NAS statement of purpose I assumed it was just a random example of widely held presuppositions. I was quite surprised, therefore, to receive the statement in an envelope mailed by a colleague at Duke asking me to become a charter member of the National Association of Scholars at Duke. I, of course, wrote to decline the honor, explaining that I could not join such an organization since it embodied presuppositions about "objectivity" that have resulted in Christian theology no longer being recognized as a legitimate academic enterprise. I find it equally problematic to think there is a set of "classics" that could be known separate from a tradition. MacIntyre's analysis in *Three Rival Versions of Moral Inquiry* seems completely confirmed by this debate.

One of the oddest set of claims I find associated with those who fear a lessening of academic rigor in the loss of something called "the canon" is their presumption that the so-called "multiculturalists," "deconstructionists" and/or "antifoundationalists" represent a politicization of the curriculum. Such a claim presumes that the curriculum was not already politicized. That people could assume that "Columbus discovered America" was objective history is but an indication that the curriculum was political. It was and is hegemonic power that could make such descriptions appear apolitical. Indeed, one of the oddities of the debate is the assumption that there is something called a canon of Western literature to be preserved. Jews and Christians rightly believe they have a canonical scripture, but I find it hard to understand how those who do not share our theological presuppositions are even using the word *canon*.

At stake in a statement of purpose like that of the NAS is the power of the "knowledge class." As Edward Said observes, "For the intellectual class, expertise has usually been a service rendered and sold to the central authority of society. This is the *trahison des clercs* of which Julien Benda spoke in the 1920s. Expertise in foreign affairs, for example, has usually meant the legitimation of foreign policy and, what is more to the point, a sustained investment in revalidating the role of experts in foreign affairs. The same sort of thing is true of literary critics and professional humanists, except that their expertise is based more upon noninterference in what Vico [eighteenth-century political philosopher] grandly calls the world of nations but which prosaically just as well be called 'the world.' We tell our students and our general constituency that we defend the classics, the virtues of liberal education, and the precious pleasures of literature, even as we show ourselves to be silent (perhaps incompetent) about the historical and social world in which things take place." *The Word, the Text, and the Critic* (Cambridge: Harvard University Press, 1983), p. 2.

21. MacIntyre identifies the encyclopediasts with Adam Gifford, Thomas Spencer Baynes, William Robertson Smith, Henry Sidgwick, D'Alembert, Diderot and, of course, Kant, among others. The great genealogist was Nietzsche, and more recently, Foucault. In many ways MacIntyre is obviously closer to the latter than to the former. I think MacIntyre is well aware of this, but he does not encourage comparison with the

antifoundationalists because he regards that position as directly correlated to the encyclopediast project. He is trying to provide a different way of reading the current debate by demonstrating that the epistemological term *philosophy* in modernity was a mistake. That is, it was a mistake to the attempt to meet the skeptic's challenge by vindicating something called rationality in general. The only way to answer the kind of skeptics created by the encyclopediast project is by showing that there is an alternative narrative. Of course that does not prohibit MacIntyre from trying to show that the genealogist may lack sufficient resources to account for themselves. That is, they cannot, given their position, show why the moral presuppositions in writing as well as reading texts can be sustained. See, for example, his arguments in *Three Rival Versions of Moral Inquiry*, pp. 52-57, pp. 196-215. MacIntyre, however, is quite aware that he can finally not provide any knock-down arguments against the genealogical project, because to try to provide such an argument would only confirm their position. John Milbank follows a very similar strategy in his *Theology and Social Theory*, pp. 278-325.

The often-made charge against the genealogists as being either nihilist or a relativist seems to me to be misplaced. Though some may be one or both, such charges in fact presuppose exactly the issues at stake. For example, the often-made claim that antifoundationalists assume that you can make anything you want from a text is simply not true. Consider, for example, Stanley Fish's account that "Interpretive communities are no more than sets of institutional practices; and while those practices are continually being transformed by the very work that they do, the transformed practice identifies itself and tells a story in relation to general purposes and goals that have survived and formed the basis of a continuity. The fact that the objects we have are all objects that appear to us in the context of some practice, of work done by some interpretive community, doesn't mean that they are not objects or that we don't have them, or that they exert no pressure on us. All it means is that they are interpreted objects and that since interpretations can change, the perceived shape of objects can change too." *Doing What Comes Naturally* (Durham: Duke University Press, 1989), p. 153. For an extremely interesting comparison of Fish and MacIntyre, see Allen Jacobs "The Unnatural Practices of Stanley Fish: A Review Essay," *South Atlantic Review* 55 (1990), pp. 87-97.

22. Lesslie Newbigin, *The Gospel in a Pluralist Society* (Grand Rapids: William B. Eerdmans Publishing, 1989).
23. James McClendon, *Systematic Theology: Ethics I* (Nashville: Abingdon Press, 1986), p. 174.
24. Newbigin, *Foolishness to the Greeks*, p. 115.
25. Newbigin, *The Gospel in a Pluralist Society*, p. 182.

Acknowledgments

Marriages are constituted by shared judgments hewn from life. Newly married, Paula and I enjoyed imaginatively exploring what we might like to do in the future. We discovered, for example, that we would like to go to Australia. We knew that was a fantasy, but fantasies are part of judgments. You can imagine our surprise when fantasy turned to possibility when out of the blue I received a letter inviting me to deliver the New College Lectures at the University of New South Wales. Possibility became reality as we went, discovering that Australia is wonderful, but the people we met there even more wonderful. There are many to thank.

I owe the trustees of the New College Lectures my thanks for the honor of inviting me to deliver the New College Lectures. I am particularly indebted to Dr. Bruce Kaye, Master of New College, for his support as well as all he taught me about the ecclesial and theological existence in Australia. He and his wife, Dr. Louise Kaye, were wonderful hosts during our stay in Sydney. We shall never forget sharing our first anniversary with Bruce and Louise during which Paula got to pet a koala (and a wombat), enjoyed a lovely picnic on the way to the Blue Mountains, and ended the day with the most spectacular sunset imaginable. It was a day of magic and friendship.

As part of my responsibilities as the New College Lecturer I was to give lectures not only in Sydney, but Canberra, Melbourne, and Perth. Wayne Hooper was our host at St. Mark's, Canberra. He organized a wonderful seminar not only with academics, but also politicians. I doubt I shall ever forget some of the exchanges we had that extraordinary morning. Dr. John Henley, a friend made previously in the States, was kind enough to bring us to Melbourne. He not only introduced us to the Melbourne zoo, but also helped us become acquainted with the wonderful ecumenical effort in theological education taking place in Melbourne. Archbishop Peter Carnley and Anne Carnley made our stay in Perth as fascinating as that city is beautiful. Thanks to them we shall never forget Australia as it is now part of our lives.

Dr. Kaye suggested that the lectures ought to deal in general with the relationship between Christianity and modernity. I appreciated such a wide open agenda but, of course, it is not easy to know what to do. In trying to conceive as well as develop that set of issues, I have been helped by many. Not the least being Dr. Kaye who has written as wisely as anyone about the peculiar challenges facing the church and that modern society known by the name of Australia.

On a more general level I obviously owe a deep debt to Alasdair MacIntyre. I always feel a bit overcome by his intelligence and erudition. I hope he will forgive my attempt to yoke his work to a position he may well disapprove. It is probably a sign of the unusual times in which we live that I can be at once influenced by Alasdair MacIntyre and John Howard Yoder without feeling a deep sense of contradiction. Professor John Milbank has also taught me much as will be apparent from the footnotes in this book. He is helping us develop a new sense of how theology might be done and I eagerly await his continuing work.

As usual I owe much to Professors Tommy Langford and Ken Surin. Tommy's wisdom and measured judgments often cause me to reconsider my more exaggerated claims. Ken Surin never fails to challenge my drift into conventionality. Will Willimon, moreover, remains one of my most valuable conversation partners and friends. Will constantly reminds me that there is nothing more intellectually demanding than the ministry of the church.

I am in Professor Greg Jones's debt for reading and criticizing the manuscript. Professor Mike Cartwright also made valuable suggestions about individual essays. Phil Kenneson read the whole manuscript and made invaluable suggestions. Actually *made invaluable suggestions* is far too weak, as he forced me through strength of argument to change my mind about some of the directions I was going. David Matzko brought his usual good sense and humor to bear on the manuscript and helped me understand what I had written in a new way. Kathy Rudy first brought my attention to the work of Catherine MacKinnon and Fritz Bauerschmidt underlined it. I continue to be gifted by many graduate students, present and graduated, who simply will not give up on their mission to educate me. I continue to be amazed by their trust and support.

Dr. Paul Franklyn of Abingdon Press from the beginning has been a wonderful supporter of this project. I wish I could have followed all of his suggestions about how the book might be better written. At least the reader should know that where the book reads well that probably owes much to Paul's hand.

As usual, of course, this book could not have seen the light of day without the extraordinary help of Gay Trotter. Her willingness to type and retype this manuscript witnesses to a patience and a spirit that humbles me. I am coming to the end of six years as Director of Graduate Studies in the Graduate Program in Religion at Duke. During that time Gay has quite literally made it possible for me to continue to write. I shall miss her support and skill, but it is good to know our friendship will remain.

Our lives are constituted by others that are graces we do not deserve but make us more than we are. My life has obviously been transformed by the love of my wife, Paula Gilbert. But good loves do not enclose but open us to others. One of the others that Paula made present was Professor Stuart Henry, her dissertation director, who is now Professor Emeritus of American Church History at the Divinity School at Duke. Over the past five years Stuart has been my great good friend and counselor. His wisdom, his eloquence, and his wonderful sense of the oddness of life has enriched Paula's and my life together in a singular fashion. It is therefore with a deep sense of gratitude and humility I dedicate this book to Dr. Stuart C. Henry.

Index